# SEEDTIME
# AND HARVEST

# SEEDTIME AND HARVEST

*A Mystical View of the Scriptures*

### Deluxe Edition

# Neville Goddard

*Includes a Biographical Essay and Timeline*
*by PEN Award-Winning Historian*

## Mitch Horowitz

**MEDIA**

Published 2022 by Gildan Media LLC
aka G&D Media
www.GandDmedia.com

Front cover design by David Rheinhardt of Pyrographx

Library of Congress Cataloging-in-Publication Data is available upon request

ISBN: 978-1-7225-0583-7

10   9   8   7   6   5   4   3   2   1

*To all of you who apply what you read in this book, and, by so doing, create a finer world.*

# CONTENTS

# I

# SEEDTIME
# AND HARVEST

# 1

# "THE END OF A GOLDEN STRING"

*"I Give you the end of a golden string;*
*Only wind it into a ball,*
*It will lead you in at Heaven's gate,*
*Built in Jerusalem's wall."*

**BLAKE**

In the following essays I have tried to indicate certain ways of approach to the understanding of the Bible and the realization of your dreams.

*"That ye be not slothful, but followers of them who*
*through faith and patience inherit the promises."*

HEBREWS 6:12

Many who enjoy the old familiar verses of Scripture are discouraged when they themselves try to read the Bible as they would any other book because, quite excusably, they do not understand that the Bible is written in the language of symbolism. Not knowing that all of its characters are personifications of the laws and functions of Mind; that the Bible is psychology rather than history, they puzzle their brains over it for awhile and then give up. It is all too mystifying. To understand the significance of its imagery, the reader of the Bible must be imaginatively awake.

According to the Scriptures, we sleep with Adam and wake with Christ. That is, we sleep collectively and wake individually.

> *"And the Lord God caused a deep sleep to fall upon*
> *Adam, and he slept."*
>
> GENESIS 2:21

If Adam, or generic man, is in a deep sleep, then his experiences as recorded in the Scriptures must be a dream. Only he who is awake can tell his dream, and only he who understands the symbolism of dreams can interpret the dream.

> *"And they said one to another, Did not our heart burn*
> *within us, while He talked with us by the way, and*
> *while He opened to us the Scriptures?"*
>
> LUKE 24:32

The Bible is a revelation of the laws and functions of Mind expressed in the language of that twilight realm into which we go when we sleep. Because the symbolical language of this twilight realm is much the same for all men, the recent explorers of this realm—human imagination—call it the "collective unconscious."

The purpose of this book, however, is not to give you a complete definition of Biblical symbols or exhaustive interpretations of its stories. All I hope to have done is to have indicated the way in which you are most likely to succeed in realizing your desires. "What things soever ye desire" can be obtained only through the conscious, voluntary exercise of imagination in direct obedience to the laws of Mind. Somewhere within this realm of imagination there is a mood, a feeling of the wish fulfilled which, if appropriated, means success to you. This realm, this Eden—your imagination—is vaster than you know and repays exploration. "I Give you the end of a golden string;" You must wind it into a ball.

# 2

# THE FOUR
# MIGHTY ONES

*"And a river went out of Eden to water the
garden; and from thence it was parted,
and became into four heads."*

**GENESIS 2:10**

*"And every one had four faces: ..."*

**EZEKIEL 10:14**

*"I see four men loose, walking in the midst
of the fire, and they have no hurt; and the
form of the fourth is like the Son of God."*

**DANIEL 3:25**

*"Four Mighty Ones are in every Man."*

**BLAKE**

The "Four Mighty Ones" constitute the selfhood of man, or God in man. There are "Four Mighty Ones" in every man, but these "Four Mighty Ones" are not four separate beings, separated one from the other as are the fingers of his hand. The "Four Mighty

Ones" are four different aspects of his mind, and differ from one another in function and character without being four separate selves inhabiting one man's body.

The "Four Mighty Ones" may be equated with the four Hebrew characters: י ח ו ה, which form the four-lettered mystery-name of the Creative Power, derived from and combining within itself the past, present and future forms of the verb "to be." The Tetragrammaton is revered as the symbol of the Creative Power in man—I AM—the creative four functions in man reaching forth to realize in actual material phenomena qualities latent in Itself.

We can best understand the "Four Mighty Ones" by comparing them to the four most important characters in the production of a play.

> "All the world's a stage,
> And all the men and women merely players; They have
> their exits and their entrances;
> And one man in his time plays many parts..."
>
> AS YOU LIKE IT: ACT II, SCENE VII

The producer, the author, the director and the actor are the four most important characters in the production of a play. In the drama of life, the producer's function is to suggest the theme of a play. This he does in the form of a wish, such as, "I wish I were successful"; "I wish I could take a trip"; "I wish I were married", and so on. But to appear on the world's stage, these general themes must somehow be specified and worked out in detail. It is not enough to say, "I wish I were successful"—that is too vague. Successful at *what?* However, the first "Mighty One" only suggests a theme.

The dramatization of the theme is left to the originality of the second "Mighty One", the author. In dramatizing the theme, the author writes only the last scene of the play—but this scene he writes in detail. The scene must dramatize the wish fulfilled. He mentally constructs as life-like a scene as possible of what he would experience had he realized his wish. When the scene is clearly visualized, the author's work is done.

The third "Mighty One" in the production of life's play is the director. The director's tasks are to see that the actor remains faithful to the script and to rehearse him over and over again until he is natural in the part. This function may be likened to a controlled and consciously directed attention—an attention focused exclusively on the action which implies that the wish is already realized.

"The form of the Fourth is like the Son of God"—human imagination, the actor. This fourth "Mighty One" performs within himself, in imagination, the pre-determined action which implies the fulfillment of the wish. This function does not visualize or observe the action. This function actually enacts the drama, and does it over and over again until it takes on the tones of reality. Without the dramatized vision of fulfilled desire, the theme remains a mere theme and sleeps forever in the vast chambers of unborn themes. Nor without the co-operant attention, obedient to the dramatized vision of fulfilled desire, will the vision perceived attain objective reality.

These "Four Mighty Ones" are the four quarters of the *human soul.* The first is Jehovah's King, who suggests the theme; the second is Jehovah's servant, who faithfully works out the theme in a dramatic vision; the third is Jehovah's man, who was attentive and obedient to the vision of fulfilled desire, who brings the wandering imagination back to the script "seventy times seven". The "Form of the Fourth" is Jehovah himself, who enacts the dramatized theme on the stage of the mind.

> *"Let this mind be in you, which was also in Christ Jesus: Who, being in the form of God, thought it not robbery to be equal with God"*
>
> PHILIPPIANS 2:5, 6

The drama of life is a joint effort of the four quarters of the human soul.

> *"All that you behold, tho' it appears without, it is within, in your imagination, of which this world of mortality is but a shadow."*
>
> BLAKE

All that we behold is a visual construction contrived to express a theme—a theme which has been dramatized, rehearsed and performed elsewhere. What we are witnessing on the stage of the world is an optical construction devised to express the themes which have been dramatized, rehearsed and performed in the imaginations of men.

These "Four Mighty Ones" constitute the Selfhood of man, or God in man; and all that man beholds, tho' it appears without, are but shadows cast upon the screen of space—optical constructions contrived by Selfhood to inform him in regard to the themes which he has conceived, dramatized, rehearsed and performed within himself.

"The creature was made subject unto vanity" that he may become conscious of Selfhood and its functions, for with consciousness of Selfhood and its functions, he can act to a purpose; he can have a consciously self-determined history. Without such consciousness, he acts unconsciously, and cries to an objective God to save him from his own creation.

> "O Lord, how long shall I cry, and Thou wilt not hear!
> even cry out unto Thee of violence, and Thou wilt not
> save!"

HABAKKUK 1:2

When man discovers that life is a play which he, himself, is consciously or unconsciously writing, he will cease from the blind, self-torture of executing judgment upon others. Instead, he will rewrite the play to conform to his ideal, for he will realize that all changes in the play must come from the cooperation of the "Four Mighty Ones" within himself. They alone can alter the script and produce the change.

All the men and women in his world are merely players and are as helpless to change his play as are the players on the screen of the theatre to change the picture. The desired change must be conceived, dramatized, rehearsed and performed in the theatre of his mind. When the fourth function, the imagination, has completed its task of rehearsing the revised version of the play until it is natural, then the curtain will rise upon this so seemingly solid world and the "Mighty Four" will cast a shadow of the real play upon the screen of space. Men and women will automatically play their parts to bring about the fulfillment of the dramatized theme. The players, by reason of their various parts in the world's drama, become relevant to the individual's dramatized theme and, because relevant, are drawn into his drama. They will play their parts, faithfully believing all the while that it was they themselves who initiated the parts they play. This they do because:

> "Thou, Father, art in me, and I in thee, . . .
> I in them, and thou in me."

>> JOHN 17:21, 23

I am involved in mankind. We are one. We are all playing the four parts of producer, author, director and actor in the drama of life. Some of us are doing it consciously, others unconsciously. It is necessary that we do it consciously. Only in this way can we be certain of a perfect ending to our play. Then we shall understand why we must become conscious of the four functions of the one God within ourselves that we may have the companionship of God as His Sons.

> "Man should not stay a man:
> His aim should higher be. For God will only gods
> Accept as company."

>> ANGELUS SILESIUS

In January of 1946, I took my wife and little daughter to Barbados in the British West Indies for a holiday. Not knowing there were any difficulties in getting a return passage, I had not booked ours before leaving New York. Upon our arrival in Barbados, I discovered that there were only two ships serving the islands, one from Boston and one from New York. I was told there was no available space on either ship before September. As I had commitments in New York for the first week in May, I put my name on the long waiting list for the April sailing.

A few days later, the ship from New York was anchored in the harbor. I observed it very carefully, and decided that this was the ship we should take. I returned to my hotel and determined on an inner action that would be mine were we actually sailing on that ship. I settled down in an easy chair in my bedroom, to lose myself in this imaginative action.

In Barbados, we take a motor launch or rowboat out into the deep harbor when we embark on a large steamer. I knew I must catch the feeling that we were sailing on that ship. I chose the inner action of stepping from the tender and climbing up the gangplank of the steamer. The first time I tried it, my attention wandered after I had reached the top of the gangplank. I brought myself back down, and tried again and again. I do not recall how many times I carried out this action in my imagination until I reached the deck and looked back at the port with the feeling of sweet sadness at departing. I was happy to be returning to my home in New York, but nostalgic in saying goodbye to the lovely island and our family and friends. I do recall that in one of my many attempts at walking up the gangplank in the feeling that I was sailing, I fell asleep. After I awoke, I went about the usual social activities of the day and evening.

The following morning, I received a call from the steamship company requesting me to come down to their office and pick up our tickets for the April sailing. I was curious to know why Barbados had been chosen to receive the cancellation and why I, at the end of the long waiting list, was to have the reservation, but all that the agent could tell me was that a cable had been received that morning from New York, offering passage for three. I was not the first the agent had called, but for reasons she could not explain, those she had called said that now they found it inconvenient to sail in April. We sailed on April 20th and arrived in New York on the morning of May the first.

In the production of my play—sailing on a boat that would bring me to New York by the first of May—I played the four most important characters in my drama. As the producer, I decided to sail on a specific ship at a certain time. Playing the part of the author, I wrote the script—I visualized the inner action which conformed to the outer action I would take if my desire were realized. As the director, I rehearsed myself, the actor, in that imagined action of climbing the gangplank until that action felt completely natural.

This being done, events and people moved swiftly to conform, in the outer world, to the play I had constructed and enacted in my imagination.

> *"I saw the mystic vision flow*
> *And live in men and woods and streams,*
> *Until I could no longer know*
> *The stream of life from my own dreams."*
>
> GEORGE WILLIAM RUSSELL (AE)

I told this story to an audience of mine in San Francisco, and a lady in the audience told me how she had unconsciously used the same technique, when she was a young girl.

The incident occurred on Christmas Eve. She was feeling very sad and tired and sorry for herself. Her father, whom she adored, had died suddenly. Not only did she feel this loss at the Christmas season, but necessity had forced her to give up her planned college years and go to work. This rainy Christmas Eve she was riding home on a San Diego street car. The car was filled with gay chatter of happy young people home for the holidays. To hide her tears from those round about her, she stood on the open part at the front of the car and turned her face into the skies to mingle her tears with the rain. With her eyes closed, and holding the rail of the car firmly, this is what she said to herself: "This is not the salt of tears that I taste, but the salt of the sea in the wind. This is not San Diego, this is the South Pacific and I am sailing into the Bay of Samoa". And looking up, in her imagination, she constructed what she imagined to be the Southern Cross. She lost herself in this contemplation so that all faded round about her. Suddenly she was at the end of the line, and home.

Two weeks later, she received word from a lawyer in Chicago that he was holding three thousand dollars in American bonds for her. Several years before, an aunt of hers had gone to Europe, with instructions that these bonds be turned over to her niece if she did not return to the United States. The lawyer had just received word of the aunt's death, and was now carrying out her instructions.

A month later, this girl sailed for the islands in the South Pacific. It was night when she entered the Bay of Samoa. Looking down, she could see the white foam like a "bone in the lady's mouth" as the ship ploughed through the waves, and brought the salt of the sea in the wind. An officer on duty said to her: "There is the Southern Cross", and looking up, she saw the Southern Cross as she had imagined it.

In the intervening years, she had many opportunities to use her imagination constructively, but as she had done this unconsciously, she did not realize there was a Law behind it all. Now that she understands, she, too, is consciously playing her four major roles in the daily drama of her life, producing plays for the good of others as well as herself.

> "Then the soldiers, when they had crucified Jesus, took
> his garments, and made four parts, to every soldier
> a part; and also his coat: now the coat was without
> seam, woven from the top throughout."
>
> JOHN 19:23

# 3

# THE GIFT OF FAITH

*"And the Lord had respect unto Abel*
*and to his offerings: But unto Cain and*
*to his offering he had not respect."*

**GENESIS 4:4, 5**

If we search the Scriptures, we will become aware of a far deeper meaning in the above quotation than that which a literal reading would give us. The Lord is none other than your own consciousness. ". . . say unto the children of Israel, I AM hath sent me unto you." (Exodus 3:14) "I AM" is the self-definition of the Lord.

Cain and Abel, as the grandchildren of the Lord, can be only personifications of two distinct functions of your own consciousness. The author is really concerned to show the "Two Contrary States of the Human Soul," and he has used two brothers to show these states. The two brothers represent two distinct outlooks on the world, possessed by everyone. One is the limited perception of the senses, and the other is an imaginative view of the world. Cain—the first view—is a passive surrender to appearances and an acceptance of life on the basis of the world without: a view which inevitably leads to unsatisfied longing or to contentment with disillusion. Abel—the second view—is a vision of fulfilled desire, lifting man above the evidence of the senses to that state of relief where he no longer pines with desire. Ignorance of the second view is a soul on fire. Knowledge of the second view is the wing whereby it flies to the Heaven of fulfilled desire.

> *"Come, eat my bread and drink of the wine that I have mingled, forsake the foolish and live."*
>
> PROVERBS 9:56

In the epistle to the Hebrews, the writer tells us that Abel's offering was faith and, states the author,

> *"Without faith it is impossible to please Him"*
>
> HEBREWS 11:6

> *"Now faith is the substance of things hoped for, the evidence of things not seen . . .*
>
> *Through faith we understand that the worlds were framed by the word of God, so that things which are seen were not made of things which do appear."*
>
> HEBREWS 11:1, 3

Cain offers the evidence of the senses which consciousness, the Lord, rejects, because acceptance of this gift as a mold of the future would mean the fixation and perpetuation of the present state forever. The sick would be sick, the poor would be poor, the thief would be a thief, the murderer a murderer, and so on, without hope of redemption.

The Lord, or consciousness, has no respect for such passive use of imagination—which is the gift of Cain. He delights in the gift of Abel, the active, voluntary, loving exercise of the imagination on behalf of man for himself and others.

> *"Let the weak man say, I am strong."*
>
> JOEL 3:10

Let man disregard appearances and declare himself to be the man he wants to be. Let him imagine beauty where his senses reveal ashes, joy where they testify to mourning, riches where they bear witness to poverty. Only by such active, voluntary use of imagination can man be lifted up and Eden restored.

The ideal is always waiting to be incarnated, but unless we ourselves offer the ideal to the Lord, our consciousness, by assuming that we are already that which we seek to embody, it is incapable of birth. The Lord needs his daily lamb of faith to mold the world in harmony with our dreams.

> *"By faith Abel offered unto God a more excellent sacrifice than Cain"*
>
> HEBREWS 11:4

Faith sacrifices the apparent fact for the unapparent truth. Faith holds fast to the fundamental truth that through the medium of an assumption, invisible states become visible facts.

> *"For what is faith unless it is to believe what you do not see?"*

> ST. AUGUSTINE

Just recently, I had the opportunity to observe the wonderful results of one who had the faith to believe what she did not see.

A young woman asked me to meet her sister and her three-year-old nephew. He was a fine, healthy lad with clear blue eyes and an exceptionally fine unblemished skin. Then, she told me her story.

At birth, the boy was perfect in every way save for a large, ugly birthmark covering one side of his face. Their doctor advised them that nothing could be done about this type of scar. Visits to many specialists only confirmed his statement. Hearing the verdict, the aunt set herself the task of proving her faith—that an assumption, though denied by the evidence of the senses, if persisted in, will harden into fact.

Every time she thought of the baby, which was often, she saw, in her imagination, an eight-month-old baby with a perfect face—without any trace of a scar. This was not easy, but she knew that in this case, that was the gift of Abel which pleased God. She persisted in her faith—she believed what was not there to be seen. The result was that she visited her sister on the child's eight-month birthday and found him to have a perfect, unblemished skin with no trace of a birthmark ever having been present. "Luck! Coincidence!" shouts Cain. No. Abel knows that these are names given by those who have no faith, to the works of faith.

*"We walk by faith, not by sight."*

II. CORINTHIANS 5:7

When reason and the facts of life oppose the idea you desire to realize and you accept the evidence of your senses and the dictates of reason as the truth, you have brought the Lord—your consciousness—the gift of Cain. It is obvious that such offerings do not please Him.

Life on earth is a training ground for image making. If you use only the molds which your senses dictate, there will be no change in your life. You are here to live the more abundant life, so you must use the invisible molds of imagination and make results and accomplishments the crucial test of your power to create. Only as you assume the feeling of the wish fulfilled and continue therein are you offering the gift that pleases.

*"When Abel's gift is my attire Then I'll realize my great desire."*

The Prophet Malachi complains that man has robbed God:

*"But ye say, Wherein have we robbed thee? In tithes
and offerings."*

MALACHI 3:8

Facts based upon reason and the evidence of the senses which
oppose the idea seeking expression, rob you of the belief in the
reality of the invisible state. But "faith is the evidence of things
not seen", and through it "God calleth those things which be not
as though they were" (Romans 4:17). Call the thing not seen;
assume the feeling of your wish fulfilled.

*" . . . that there may be meat in mine house, and prove me
now herewith, sayeth the Lord of hosts, if I will not open
you the windows of heaven, and pour you out a blessing,
that there shall not be room enough to receive it."*

MALACHI 3:10

This is the story of a couple living in Sacramento, California,
who refused to accept the evidence of their senses, who refused
to be robbed, in spite of a seeming loss. The wife had given her
husband a very valuable wristwatch. The gift doubled its value
because of the sentiment he attached to it. They had a little ritual
with the watch. Every night as he removed the watch he gave it to
her and she put it away in a special box in the bureau. Every morning she took the watch and gave it to him to put on.

One morning the watch was missing. They both remembered
playing their usual parts the night before, therefore the watch

was not lost or misplaced, but stolen. Then and there, they determined not to accept the fact that it was really gone. They said to each other, "This is an opportunity to practice what we believe." They decided that, in their imagination, they would enact their customary ritual as though the watch were actually there. In his imagination, every night the husband took off the watch and gave it to his wife, while in her imagination she accepted the watch and carefully put it away. Every morning she removed the watch from its box and gave it to her husband and he, in turn, put it on. This they did faithfully for two weeks.

After their fourteen-day vigil, a man went into the one and only jewelry store in Sacramento where the watch would be recognized. As he offered a gem for appraisal, the owner of the store noticed the wristwatch he was wearing. Under the pretext of needing a closer examination of the stone, he went into an inner office and called the police. After the police arrested the man, they found in his apartment over ten thousand dollars worth of stolen jewelry. In walking "by faith, not by sight", this couple attained their desire—the watch—and also aided many others in regaining what had seemed to be lost forever.

> "If one advances confidently in the direction of his dream, and endeavors to live the life which he has imagined, he will meet with a success unexpected in common hours."
>
> THOREAU

# 4

# THE SCALE OF BEING

*"And he dreamed, and behold a ladder set up on
the earth, and the top of it reached to heaven: and
behold the angels of God ascending and descending
on it. And, behold, the Lord stood above it . . ."*

**GENESIS 28:12, 13**

In a dream, in a vision of the night, when deep sleep fell upon
Jacob, his inner eye was opened and he beheld the world as a series
of ascending and descending levels of awareness. It was a revelation
of the deepest insight into the mysteries of the world. Jacob saw a
vertical scale of ascending and descending values, or states of consciousness. This gave meaning to everything in the outer world, for
without such a scale of values there would be no meaning to life.

At every moment of time, man stands upon the eternal scale of
meaning. There is no object or event that has ever taken place or is
taking place now that is without significance. The significance of
an object or event for the individual is a direct index to the level of
his consciousness.

You are holding this book, for example. On one level of consciousness, it is an object in space. On a higher level, it is a series

of letters on paper, arranged according to certain rules. On a still higher level, it is an expression of meaning.

Looking outwardly, you see the book first, but actually, the meaning comes first. It occupies a higher grade of significance than the letter arrangement on paper or the book as an object in space. Meaning determined the arrangement of letters; the arrangement of letters only expresses the meaning. The meaning is invisible and above the level of the visible arrangement of letters. If there had been no meaning to be expressed, no book would have been written and published.

*"And, behold, the Lord stood above it . . ."*

The Lord and meaning are one—the Creator, the cause of the phenomena of life.

> *"In the beginning was the Word, and the Word was*
> *with God, and the Word was God."*
>
> JOHN 1:1

In the beginning was the intention—the meaning—and the intention was with the intender, and the intention *was* the intender. The objects and events in time and space occupy a lower level of significance than the level of meaning which produced them. All things were made by meaning, and without meaning was not anything made that was made. The fact that everything seen can be regarded as the effect, on a lower level of significance, of an unseen higher order of significance is a very important one to grasp.

Our usual mode of procedure is to attempt to explain the higher levels of significance—why things happen—in terms of the lower levels—what and how things happen. For example, let us take an actual accident and try to explain it.

Most of us live on the level of what happened—the accident was an event in space—one automobile struck another and practically demolished it. Some of us live on the higher level of "how" the accident happened—it was a rainy night, the roads were slippery and the second car skidded into the first. On rare occasions, a few of us reach the highest or causal level of "why" such an accident occurs. Then we become aware of the invisible, the state of consciousness which produced the visible event.

In this case, the ruined car was driven by a widow, who, though she felt she could not afford to, greatly desired to change her environment. Having heard that, by the proper use of her imagination, she could do and be all she wished to be, this widow had been imagining herself actually living in the city of her desire. At the same time, she was living in a consciousness of loss, both personal and financial. Therefore, she brought upon herself an event which was seemingly another loss, but the sum of money the insurance company paid her allowed her to make the desired change in her life.

When we see the "why" behind the seeming accident, the state of consciousness that produced the accident, we are led to the conclusion that there is no accident. Everything in life has its invisible meaning.

The man who learns of an accident, the man who knows "how" it happened, and the man who knows "why" it happened are on three different levels of awareness in regard to that accident. On the ascending scale, each higher level carries us a step in advance towards the truth of the accident.

We should strive constantly to lift ourselves to the higher level of meaning, the meaning that is always invisible and above the physical event. But, remember, the meaning or cause of the phenomena of life can be found only within the consciousness of man.

Man is so engrossed in the visible side of the drama of life—the side of "what" has happened, and "how" it happened—that he rarely rises to the invisible side of "why" it happened. He refuses to accept the Prophet's warning that:

> *"Things which are seen were not made of things that do appear."*
>
> HEBREWS 11:3

His descriptions of "what" has happened and "how" it happened are true in terms of his corresponding level of thought, but when he asks "why" it happened, all physical explanations break down and he is forced to seek the "why", or meaning of it, on the invisible and higher level. The mechanical analysis of events deals only with external relationships of things. Such a course will never reach the level which holds the secret of *why* the events happen. Man must recognize that the lower and visible sides flow from the invisible and higher level of meaning.

Intuition is needed to lift us up to the level of meaning—to the level of *why* things happen. Let us follow the advice of the Hebrew prophet of old and "lift up our eyes unto the hills" within ourselves, and observe what is taking place there. See what ideas we have accepted as true, what states we have consented to, what dreams, what desires—and, above all, what intentions. It is from these hills that all things come to reveal our stature—our height—on the vertical scale of meaning. If we lift our eyes to "the Thee in Me who works behind the Veil", we will see the meaning of the phenomena of life.

Events appear on the screen of space to express the different levels of consciousness of man. A change in the level of his consciousness automatically results in a change of the phenomena of his life. To attempt to change conditions before he changes the level of consciousness from whence they came, is to struggle in vain. Man redeems the world as he ascends the vertical scale of meaning.

We saw, in the analogy of the book that as consciousness was lifted up to the level where man could see meaning expressed in the arrangement of its letters, it also included the knowledge that the letters were arranged according to certain rules, and that such arrangements, when printed on paper and bound together, formed a book. What is true of the book is true of every event in the world.

> "They shall not hurt nor destroy in all my holy
> mountain: for the earth shall be full of the knowledge
> of the Lord, as the waters cover the sea."

ISAIAH 11:9

Nothing is to be discarded; all is to be redeemed. Our lives, ascending the vertical scale of meaning towards an ever increasing awareness—an awareness of things of higher significance—are the process whereby this redemption is brought to pass. As man arranges letters into words, and words into sentences to express meaning, in like manner, life arranges circumstances, conditions and events to express the unseen meanings or attitudes of men. Nothing is without significance. But man, not knowing the higher level of inner meaning, looks out upon a moving panorama of events and sees no meaning to life. There is always a level of meaning determining events and their essential relationship to our lives.

Here is a story that will enable us to seize the good in things seeming evil; to withhold judgment, and to act aright amid unsolved problems.

Just a few years ago, our country was shocked by a seeming injustice in our midst. The story was told on radio and television, as well as in the newspapers. You may recall the incident. The body of a young American soldier killed in Korea was returned to his home for burial. Just before the service, his wife was asked a routine question: Was her husband a Caucasian? When she replied that he was an Indian, burial was refused. This refusal was in accordance with the laws of that community, but it aroused the entire nation. We felt incensed that anyone who had been killed in the service of his country should be denied burial anywhere in his country. The story reached the attention of the President of the United States, and he offered burial with full military honors in Arlington National Cemetery. After the service, the wife told reporters that her husband had always dreamed of dying a hero, and having a hero's burial service with full military honors.

When, we in America, had to explain why progressive, intelligent people like ourselves, not only enacted but supported such laws in our great land of the free and the brave, we were hard put for an explanation. We, as observers, had seen only "what" happened, and "how" it happened. We failed to see "why" it happened.

That burial *had* to be refused if that lad was to realize his dream. We tried to explain the drama in terms of the lower level of "how" it happened, which explanation could not satisfy the one who had asked "why" it happened.

The true answer, viewed from the level of higher meaning, would be such a reversal of our common habits of thinking that it would be instantly rejected. The truth is that future states are causative of present facts—the Indian boy dreaming of a hero's death, with full military honors, was like Lady Macbeth transported "beyond this ignorant present", and could "feel now the future in the instant."

*". . . and by it he being dead yet speaketh."*

HEBREWS 11:4

# 5

# THE GAME OF LIFE

*"I can easier teach twenty what were good
to be done, than be one of the twenty
to follow mine own teaching."*

**SHAKESPEARE**

With this confession off my mind, I will now teach you how to play the game of life. Life is a game and, like all games, it has its aims and its rules.

In the little games that men concoct, such as cricket, tennis, baseball, football, and so on, the rules may be changed from time to time. After the changes are agreed upon, man must learn the new rules and play the game within the framework of the accepted rules.

However, in the game of life, the rules cannot be changed or broken. Only within the framework of its universal and everlastingly fixed rules can the game of life be played.

The game of life is played on the playing field of the mind. In playing a game, the first thing we ask is, "What is its aim and purpose?" and the second, "What are the rules governing the game?" In the game of life, our chief aim is towards increasing awareness—an awareness of things of greater significance; and our second aim is towards achieving our goals, realizing our desires.

As to our desires, the rules reach only so far as to indicate the way in which we should go to realize them, but the desires themselves must be the individual's own concern. The rules governing the game of life are simple, but it takes a lifetime of practice to use them wisely. Here is one of the rules:

*"As he thinketh in his heart, so is he."*

PROVERBS 23:7

Thinking is usually believed to be a function entirely untrammeled and free, without any rules to constrain it. But that is not true. Thinking moves by its own processes in a bounded territory, with definite paths and patterns.

ᶲ

**"Thinking follows the tracks laid down in one's own inner conversations."**

All of us can realize our objectives by the wise use of *mind* and *speech*. Most of us are totally unaware of the mental activity which goes on within us. But to play the game of life successfully, we must become aware of our every mental activity, for this activity, in the form of inner conversations, is the cause of the outer phenomena of our life.

*"... every idle word that man shall speak, they shall give account thereof in the day of judgment.*

*For by thy words thou shalt be justified, and by thy words thou shalt be condemned."*

MATTHEW 12:36, 37

The law of the Word cannot be broken.

*"... A bone of him shall not be broken."*

JOHN 19:36

The law of the Word never overlooks an inner word nor makes the smallest allowance for our ignorance of its power. It fashions life about us as we, by our inner conversations, fashion life within ourselves. This is done to reveal to us our position on the playing field of life. There is no opponent in the game of life; there is only the goal.

Not long ago, I was discussing this with a successful and philanthropic business man. He told me a thought-provoking story about himself.

He said, "You know, Neville, I first learned about goals in life when I was fourteen, and it was on the playing field at school. I was good at track and had had a fine day, but there was one more race to run and I had stiff competition in one other boy. I was determined to beat him. I beat him, it is true, but, while I was keeping my eye on him, a third boy, who was considered no competition at all, won the race.

"That experience taught me a lesson I have used throughout my life. When people ask me about my success, I must say, that I believe it is because I have never made 'making money' my goal: 'My goal is the wise, productive use of money.'"

This man's inner conversations are based on the premise that he already has money, his constant inner question: the proper use of it. The inner conversations of the man struggling to "get" money only prove his lack of money. In his ignorance of the power of the word, he is building barriers in the way of the attainment of his goal; he has his eye on the competition rather than on the goal itself.

> *"The fault, dear Brutus, is not in our stars, But in*
> *ourselves, that we are underlings."*
>
> *JULIUS CAESAR:* ACT 1, SCENE II

As "the worlds were framed by the Word of God", so we as "imitators of God as dear children" create the conditions and circumstances of our lives by our all-powerful human inner words. Without practice, the most profound knowledge of the game would produce no desired results. "To him that knoweth to do good"—that is, knoweth the rules—"and doeth it not, to him it is sin". In other words, he will miss his mark and fail to realize his goal. In the parable of the Talents, the Master's condemnation of the servant who neglected to use his gift is clear and unmistakable, and having discovered one of the rules of the game of life, we risk failure by ignoring it. The talent not used, like the limb not exercised, slumbers and finally atrophies. We must be "doers of the Word, and not hearers only". Since thinking follows the tracks laid down in one's own inner conversations, not only can we see where we are going on the playing field of life by observing our inner conversations, but also, we can determine where we will go by controlling and directing our inner talking.

What would you think and say and do were you already the one you want to be? Begin to think and say and do this inwardly. You are told that "there is a God in heaven that revealeth secrets," and, you must always remember that *heaven is within you;* and to make it crystal clear who God is, where He is, and what His secrets are, Daniel continues, "Thy dream, and the visions of thy head are these". They reveal the tracks to which you are tied, and point the direction in which you are going.

This is what one woman did to turn the tracks to which she had been unhappily tied in the direction in which she wanted to go. For two years, she had kept herself estranged from the three people she loved most. She had had a quarrel with her daughter-in-law, who ordered her from her home. For those two years, she had not seen or heard from her son, her daughter-in-law or her grandson, though she had sent her grandson numerous gifts in the meantime. Every time she thought of her family, which was daily, she carried on a mental conversation with her daughter-in-law, blaming her for the quarrel and accusing her of being selfish.

Upon hearing a lecture of mine one night—it was this very lecture on the game of life and how to play it—she suddenly realized she was the cause of the prolonged silence and that she, and she alone, must do something about it. Recognizing that her goal was to have the former loving relationship, she set herself the task of completely changing her inner talking.

That very night, in her imagination, she constructed two loving, tender letters written to her, one from her daughter-in-law and the other from her grandson. In her imagination, she read them over and over again until she fell asleep in the joyful mood of having received the letters. She repeated this imaginary act each night for eight nights. On the morning of the ninth day, she received one envelope containing two letters, one from her daughter-in-law, one from her grandson. They were loving, tender letters inviting her to visit them, almost replicas of those she had constructed mentally. By using her imagination consciously and lovingly, she had turned the tracks to which she was tied, in the direction she wanted to go, towards a happy family reunion.

A change of attitude is a change of position on the playing field of life. The game of life is not being played out there in what is called space and time; the real moves in the game of life take place within, on the playing field of the mind.

> "Losing thy soul, thy soul Again to find;
> Rendering toward that goal Thy separate mind."
>
> LAURENCE HOUSMAN

# 6

# "TIME, TIMES, AND AN HALF"

*"And one said to the man clothed in linen,
which was upon the waters of the river, How
long shall it be to the end of these wonders?*

*"And I heard the man clothed in linen, which
was upon the waters of the river, when he held
up his right hand and his left hand unto heaven,
and swear by him that liveth forever that it
shall be for a time, times, and an half."*

DANIEL 12:6, 7

At one of my lectures given in Los Angeles on the subject of the hidden meaning behind the stories of the Bible, someone asked me to interpret the above quotation from the Book of Daniel. After I confessed I did not know the meaning of that particular passage, a lady in the audience said to herself, "If the mind behaves according to the assumption with which it starts, then I will find the true answer to that question and tell it to Neville." And this is what she told me.

"Last night the question was asked: 'What is the meaning of "time, times, and an half" as recorded in Daniel 12:7?'. Before going to sleep last night I said to myself, 'Now there is a simple answer to this question, so I will assume that I know it and while I am sleeping my greater self will find the answer and reveal it to my lesser self in dream or vision.'

"Around five A.M. I awakened. It was too early to rise, so remaining in bed I quickly fell into that half dreamy state between waking and sleeping, and while in that state a picture came into my mind of an old lady. She was sitting in a rocking chair and rocking back and forth, back and forth. Then a voice which sounded like your voice said to me: 'Do it over and over and over again until it takes on the tones of reality.'

"I jumped out of bed and re-read the Twelfth Chapter of Daniel, and this is the intuitive answer I received. Taking the sixth and seventh verses, for they constituted last night's question, I felt that if the garments with which Biblical characters are clothed correspond to their level of consciousness, as you teach, then linen must represent a very high level of consciousness indeed, for the 'man clothed in linen' was standing 'upon the waters of the river' and if, as you teach, water symbolizes a high level of psychological truth, then the individual who could walk upon it must truly represent an exalted state of consciousness. I therefore felt that what he had to say must indeed be very significant. Now the question asked of him was 'How long shall it be to the end of these wonders?' And his answer was, 'A time, times, and an half.' Remembering my vision of the old lady rocking back and forth, and your voice telling me to 'do it over and over and over again until it takes on the tones of reality', and remembering that this vision and your instruction came to me in response to my assumption that I knew the answer, I intuitively felt that the question asked the 'man clothed in linen' meant how long shall it be until the wonderful dreams that I am dreaming become a reality. And his answer is, 'Do it over and over and over again until it takes on the tones of reality'. 'A time' means to perform the imaginary action which implies the fulfillment of the wish; 'Times' mean to repeat the imaginary action over and over again, and 'an half' means the moment of falling asleep while performing the imaginary action, for such a moment usually arrives before the pre-determined action is completed and, there-fore, can be said to be a half, or part, of a time."

To get such inner understanding of the Scriptures by the sim-ple assumption that she did know the answer, was a wonderful experience for this woman. However, to know the true meaning of "time, times, and an half" she must apply her understanding in her daily life. We are never at a loss in an opportunity to test this understanding, either for ourselves or for another.

A number of years ago, a widow living in the same apartment house as we, came to see me about her cat. The cat was her con-stant companion and dear to her heart. He was, however, eight years old, very ill and in great pain. He had not eaten for days and would not move from under her bed. Two veterinarians had seen the cat and advised the woman that the cat could not be cured, and that he should be put to sleep immediately. I suggested that that night, before retiring, she create in her imagination some action that would indicate the cat was its former healthy self. I advised her to do it over and over again until it took on the tones of reality.

This, she promised to do. However, either from lack of faith in my advice or from lack of faith in her own ability to carry out the imaginary action, she asked her niece to spend the night with her. This request was made so that if the cat were not well by morning, the niece could take it to the veterinarian's and she, the owner, would not have to face such a dreaded task herself. That night, she settled herself in an easy chair and began to imagine the cat was romping beside her, scratching at the furniture and doing many things she would not normally have allowed. Each time she found that her mind had wandered from its pre-determined task to see a normal, healthy, frisky cat, she brought her attention back to the room and started her imaginary action over again. This she did over and over again until, finally, in a feeling of relief, she dropped off to sleep, still seated in her chair.

At about four o'clock in the morning, she was awakened by the cry of her cat. He was standing by her chair. After attracting her attention, he led her to the kitchen where he begged for food. She fixed him a little warm milk which he quickly drank, and cried for more.

That cat lived comfortably for five more years, when, without pain or illness, he died naturally in his sleep.

> "How long shall it be to the end of these wonders? . . .
> A time, times, and an half.

*In a dream in a vision of the night, when deep sleep falleth upon men, in slumberings upon the bed;*

*Then he openeth the ears of men, and sealeth their instructions."*

JOB 33:15, 16

# 7

# BE YE WISE
# AS SERPENTS

*". . . be ye therefore wise as serpents,
and harmless as doves."*

**MATTHEW 10:16**

The serpent's ability to form its skin by ossifying a portion of itself, and its skill in shedding each skin as it outgrew it, caused man to regard this reptile as a symbol of the power of endless growth and self-reproduction. Man is told, therefore, to be "wise as the serpent" and learn how to shed his skin—his environment—which is his solidified self; man must learn how to "loose him, and let him go" . . . how to "put off the old man" . . . how to die to the old and yet know, like the serpent, that he "shall not surely die".

Man has not learned as yet that all that is outside his physical body is also a part of himself, that his world and all the conditions of his life are but the outpicturing of his state of consciousness. When he *knows* this truth, he will stop the futile struggle of self-contention and, like the serpent, let the old go and grow a new environment.

*"Man is immortal; therefore he must die endlessly.
For life is a creative idea; it can only find itself in
changing forms."*

TAGORE

In ancient times, serpents were also associated with the guardianship of treasure or wealth. The injunction to be "wise as serpents" is the advice to man to awaken the power of his subtilized body—his imagination—that he, like the serpent, may grow and outgrow, die and yet not die, for from such deaths and resurrections alone, shedding the old and putting on the new, shall come fulfillment of his dreams and the finding of his treasures. As "the serpent was more subtil than any beast of the field which the Lord God had made" (Genesis: 3:1)—even so, imagination is more subtile than any creature of the heavens which the Lord God had created. Imagination is the creature that:

*" . . . was made subject to vanity, not willingly, but by
reason of him who hath subjected the same in hope. . . .*

*For we are saved by hope: but hope that is seen is
not hope: for what a man seeth, why doth he yet hope
for? But if we hope for that we see not, then do we with
patience wait for it."*

ROMANS 8:20, 24, 25

Although the outer, or "natural", man of the senses is interlocked with his environment, the inner, or spiritual, man of imagination is not thus interlocked. If the interlocking were complete, the charge to be "wise as serpents" would be in vain. Were we completely inter locked with our environment, we could not withdraw our attention from the evidence of the senses and feel ourselves into the situation of our fulfilled desire, in hope that that unseen state would solidify as our new environment. But:

> *"There is a natural body, and there is a spiritual body."*
>
> I. CORINTHIANS 15:44

The spiritual body of imagination is not interlocked with man's environment. The spiritual body can withdraw from the outer man of sense and environment and imagine itself to be what it wants to be. And if it remains faithful to the vision, imagination will build for man a new environment in which to live. This is what is meant by the statement:

> *". . . I go to prepare a place for you.*
> *And if I go and prepare a place for you, I will come again, and receive you unto myself; that where I am, there ye may be also."*
>
> JOHN 14:2, 3

The place that is prepared for you need not be a place in space. It can be health, wealth, companionship, anything that you desire in this world. Now, how is the place prepared?

You must first construct as life-like a representation as possible of what you would see and hear and do if you were physically present and physically moving about in that "place". Then, with your physical body immobilized, you must imagine that you are actually in that "place" and are seeing and hearing and doing all that you would see and hear and do if you were there physically. This you must do over and over again until it takes on the tones of reality. When it feels natural, the "place" has been prepared as the new environment for your outer or physical self. Now you may open your physical eyes and return to your former state. The "place" is prepared, and where you have been in imagination, there you shall be in the body also.

How this imagined state is realized physically is not the concern of you, the natural or outer man. The spiritual body, on its return from the imagined state to its former physical state, created an invisible bridge of incident to link the two states. Although the curious feeling that you were actually there and that the state was real is gone, as soon as you open your eyes upon the old familiar environment, nevertheless, you are haunted with the sense of a double identity—with the knowledge that "there is a natural body, and there is a spiritual body." When you, the natural man, have had this experience you will go automatically across the bridge of events which leads to the physical realization of your invisibly prepared place.

This concept—that man is dual and that the inner man of imagination can dwell in future states and return to the present moment with a bridge of events to link the two—clashes violently with the widely accepted view about the human personality, and the cause and nature of phenomena. Such a concept demands a revolution in current ideas about the human personality, and about space, time and matter. The concept that man, consciously or unconsciously, determines the conditions of life by imagining himself into these mental states, leads to the conclusion that this supposedly solid world is a construction of Mind—a concept which, at first, common sense rejects. However, we should remember that most of the concepts which common sense at first rejected, man was afterward forced to accept. These never-ending reversals of judgment which experience has forced upon man led Professor Whitehead to write: "Heaven knows what seeming nonsense may not tomorrow be demonstrated truth".

The creative power in man sleeps and needs to be awakened.

> *"Awake thou that sleepest, and arise from the dead."*
> EPHESIANS 5:14

Wake from the sleep that tells you the outer world is the cause of the conditions of your life. Rise from the dead past and create a new environment.

> *"Know ye not that ye are the temple of God, and that the Spirit of God dwelleth in you?"*
> I. CORINTHIANS 3:16.

The Spirit of God in you is your imagination, but it sleeps and needs to be awakened, in order to lift you off the bar of the senses where you have so long lain stranded.

The boundless possibilities open to you as you become "wise as serpents" is beyond measure. You will select the ideal conditions you want to experience and the ideal environment you want to live in. Experiencing these states in imagination until they have sensory vividness, you will externalize them as surely as the serpent now externalizes its skin. After you have outgrown them, then, you will cast them off as easily as "the snake throws her enamell'd skin". The more abundant life—the whole purpose of Creation—cannot be save through death and resurrection.

God desired form, so He became man; and it is not enough for us to recognize His spirit at work in creation, we must see His work in form and say that it is good, even though we outgrow the form, forever and ever.

> "He leads
> Through widening chambers of delight to where Throbs
> rapture near an end that aye recedes,
> Because His touch is Infinite and lends
> A yonder to all ends."

⚘

*"And, I, if I be lifted up from the earth,*
*will draw all men unto me."*

JOHN 12:32

If I be lifted up from the evidence of the senses to the state of consciousness I desire to realize and remain in that state until it feels natural, I will form that state around me and all men will see it. But how to persuade man this is true—that imaginative life is the only living; that assuming the feeling of the wish fulfilled is the way to the more abundant life and not the compensation of the escapist—that is the problem. To see as "through widening chambers of delight" what living in the realms of imagination means, to appreciate and enjoy the world, one must live imaginatively; one must dream and occupy his dream, then grow and outgrow the dream, forever and ever. The unimaginative man, who will not lose his life on one level that he may find it on a higher level, is nothing but a Lot's wife—a pillar of self-satisfied salt. On the other hand, those who refuse form as being unspiritual and who reject incarnation as separate from God are ignorant of the great mystery: "Great is the mystery, God was manifest in the flesh."

Your life expresses one thing, and one thing only, your *state of consciousness*. Everything is dependent upon that. As you, through the medium of imagination, assume a state of consciousness, that state begins to clothe itself in form. It solidifies around you as the serpent's skin ossifies around it. But you must be faithful to the state.

You must not go from state to state, but, rather, wait patiently in the one invisible state until it takes on form and becomes an objective fact. Patience is necessary, but patience will be easy after your first success in shedding the old and growing the new, for we are able to wait according as we have been rewarded by understanding in the past. Understanding is the secret of patience. What natural joy and spontaneous delight lie in seeing the world—not with, but as Blake says—*through* the eye! Imagine that you are seeing what you want to see, and remain faithful to your vision. Your imagination will make for itself a corresponding form in which to live.

All things are made by imagination's power. Nothing begins except in the imagination of man. "From within out" is the law of the universe. "As within, so without." Man turns outward in his search for truth, but the essential thing is to look within.

> *"Truth is within ourselves; it takes no rise*
> *From outward things, what e'er you may believe. There*
> *is an inmost center in us all,*
> *Where truth abides in fullness . . . and to know,*
> *Rather consists in opening out a way*
> *Whence the imprisoned splendor may escape, Than in*
> *effecting entry for a light*
> *Supposed to be without."*
>
> BROWNING: "PARACELSUS"

I think you will be interested in an instance of how a young woman shed the skin of resentment and put on a far different kind of skin. The parents of this woman had separated when she was six years old and she had lived with her mother. She rarely saw her father. But once a year he sent her a five dollar check for Christmas. Following her marriage, he did increase the Christmas gift to ten dollars.

After one of my lectures, she was dwelling on my statement that man's suspicion of another is only a measure of his own deceitfulness, and she recognized that she had been harboring a resentment towards her father for years. That night she resolved to let go her resentment and put a fond reaction in its place. In her imagination, she felt she was embracing her father in the warmest way. She did it over and over again until she caught the spirit of her imaginary act, and then she fell asleep in a very contented mood.

The following day she happened to pass through the fur department of one of our large stores in California. For some time she had been toying with the idea of having a new fur scarf, but felt she could not afford it. This time her eye was caught by a stone marten scarf, and she picked it up and tried it on. After feeling it and seeing herself in it, reluctantly she took off the scarf and returned it to the salesman, telling herself she really could not afford it. As she was leaving the department, she stopped and thought, "Neville tells us we can have whatever we desire if we will only capture the feeling of already having it." In her imagination, she put the scarf back on, felt the reality of it, and went about her shopping, all the while enjoying the imagined wearing of it.

This young woman never associated these two imaginary acts. In fact, she had almost forgotten what she had done until, a few weeks later, on Mother's Day, the doorbell rang unexpectedly. There was her father. As she embraced him, she remembered her first imaginary action. As she opened the package he had brought her—the first gift in these many years—she remembered her second imaginary action, for the box contained a beautiful stone marten scarf.

> *"Ye are gods; and all of you are children of the most High."*
>
> PSALMS 82:6

> *"... be ye therefore wise as serpents, and harmless as doves."*
>
> MATTHEW 10:16

# 8

# THE WATER
# AND THE BLOOD

*"... Except a man be born again he*
*cannot see the kingdom of God."*

**JOHN 3:3**

*"But one of the soldiers with a spear pierced his side,*
*and forthwith came there out blood and water."*

**JOHN 19:34**

*"This is he that came by water and blood, even Jesus*
*Christ; not by water only, but by water and blood."*

**JOHN 5:6**

According to the Gospel and the Epistle of John, not only must man be "born again" but he must be "born again" of water and blood. These two inward experiences are linked with two outward rites—baptism and communion. But the two outward rites—baptism to symbolize birth by water, and the wine of communion to symbolize acceptance of the blood of the Saviour, cannot produce the real birth or radical transformation of the individual, which is promised to man. The outward use of water and wine cannot bring about the desired change of mind. We must, therefore, look for the hidden meaning behind the symbols of water and blood.

The Bible uses many images to symbolize Truth, but the images used symbolize Truth on different levels of meaning. On the lowest level, the image used is stone. For example:

> "... a great stone was upon the well's mouth. And
> thither were all the flocks gathered: and they rolled the
> stone from the well's mouth, and watered the sheep ..."
>
> GENESIS 29:2, 3

> "... they sank into the bottom as a stone."
>
> EXODUS 15:5

When a stone blocks the well, it means that people have taken these great symbolical revelations of Truth literally. When someone rolls the stone away, it means that an individual has discovered beneath the allegory or parable its psychological life germ, or meaning. This hidden meaning which lies behind the literal words is symbolized by water. It is this water, in the form of psychological Truth, that he then offers to humanity.

> "The flock of my pasture, are men."
>
> EZEKIEL 34:31

The literal-minded man who refuses the "cup of water"—psychological Truth—offered him, "sinks into the bottom as a stone". He remains on the level where he sees everything in pure objectivity, without any subjective relationship. He may keep all the Commandments—written on stone—literally, and yet break them psychologically all day long. He may, for example, not literally steal the property of another, and yet see the other in want. To see another in want, is to rob him of his birthright as a child of God. For we are all "children of the Most High."

> "And if children, then heirs; heirs of God, and joint-heirs with Christ . . ."
>
> ROMANS 8:17

To know what to do about a seeming misfortune is to have the "cup of water"—the psychological Truth—that could save the situation. But such knowledge is not enough. Man must not only "fill the water pots of *stone* with *water*"—that is, discover the psychological truth behind the obvious fact, but he must turn the water—the psychological truth—into wine. This he does by living a life according to the truth which he has discovered. Only by such use of the truth can he "taste the water that was made wine" (John 2:9).

A man's birthright is to be Jesus. He is born to "save his people from their sins" (Matthew: 1: 21). But the salvation of a man is "not by water only, but by water and blood".

To know what to do to save yourself or another is not enough; you must do it. Knowledge of what to do is *water*; doing it is *blood*.

"This is he that came not by water only, but by water and blood." The whole of this mystery is in the conscious, active use of imagination to appropriate that particular state of consciousness that would save you or another from the present limitation. Outward ceremonies cannot accomplish this.

> " . . . there shall meet you a man bearing a pitcher of water: follow him.
>
> "And wheresoever he shall go in, say ye to the goodman of the house, The Master saith, Where is the guest-chamber, where I shall eat the passover with my disciples?
>
> "And he will show you a large upper room furnished and prepared: there make ready for us."
>
> MARK 14:13, 14, 15

Whatever you desire is already "furnished and prepared". Your imagination can put you in touch inwardly with that state of consciousness. If you imagine that you are already the one you want to be, you are following the "man bearing a pitcher of water". If you remain in that state, you have entered the guest-chamber—passover—and committed your spirit into the Hands of God—your consciousness.

A man's state of consciousness is his demand on the Infinite Store House of God, and, like the law of commerce, a demand creates a supply. To change the supply, you change the demand—your state of consciousness. What you desire to be, that you must feel you already are. Your state of consciousness creates the conditions of your life, rather than the conditions create your state of consciousness. To know this Truth, is to have the "water of life".

But your Saviour—the solution of your problem—cannot be manifested by such knowledge only. It can be realized only as such knowledge is applied. Only as you assume the feeling of your wish fulfilled, and continue therein, is your "side pierced; from whence cometh blood and water". In this manner only is Jesus—the solution of your problem—realized.

> "For thou must know that in the government of thy
> mind thou art thine own lord and master, that there
> will rise up no fire in the circle or whole circumference
> of thy body and spirit, unless thou awakest it thyself."
>
> JACOB BOEHME

God is your consciousness. His promises are conditional. Unless the demand—your state of consciousness—is changed, the supply—the present conditions of your life—remain as they are. "As we forgive"—as we change our mind—the Law is automatic. Your state of consciousness is the spring of action, the directing force, and that which creates the supply.

> "If that nation, against whom I have pronounced, turn
> from their evil, I will repent of the evil that I thought to
> do unto them.

> "And at what instant I shall speak concerning a
> nation, and concerning a kingdom, to build and to
> plant it;
> "If it do evil in my sight, that it obey not my voice,
> then I will repent of the good, wherewith I said I would
> benefit them."
>
> JEREMIAH 18:8, 9, 10

This statement of Jeremiah suggests that a commitment is involved if the individual or nation would realize the goal—a commitment to certain fixed attitudes of mind. The feeling of the wish fulfilled is a necessary condition in man's search for the goal.

The story I am about to tell you shows that man is what the observer has the capacity to see in him; that what he is seen to be is a direct index to the *observer's* state of consciousness. This story is, also, a challenge to us all to "shed our blood"—use our imagination lovingly on behalf of another.

There is no day that passes that does not afford us the opportunity to transform a life by the "shedding of our blood".

> "Without the shedding of blood there is no remission."
>
> HEBREWS 9:22

One night in New York City I was able to unveil the mystery of the "water and the blood" to a school teacher. I had quoted the above statement from Hebrews 9:22, and went on to explain that the realization that we have no hope save in ourselves is the discovery that God is within us—that this discovery causes the dark caverns of the skull to grow luminous, and we *know* that: "The spirit of man is the candle of the Lord" Proverbs 20:27—and that this realization is the light to guide us safely over the earth.

> *"His candle shined upon my head and by his light I*
> *walked through darkness."*
>
> JOB 29:3

However, we must not look upon this radiant light of the head as God, for man is the image of God.

> *"God appears, and God is Light,*
> *To those poor souls who dwell in Night;*
> *But does a Human Form display*
> *To those who dwell in realms of Day."*
>
> BLAKE

But this must be experienced to be known. There is no other way, and no other man's experience can be a substitute for our own.

I told the teacher that her change of attitude in regard to another would produce a corresponding change in the other; that such *knowledge* was the true meaning of the *water* mentioned in I. John 5:6, but that such knowledge alone was not enough to produce the re-birth desired: that such re-birth could only come to pass by "water and blood", or the application of this truth. Knowledge of what to do is the *water of life*, but doing it is the *blood of the Saviour*. In other words, a little knowledge, if carried out in action is more profitable than much knowledge which we neglect to carry out in action.

As I talked, one student kept impinging upon the teacher's mind. But this, thought she, would be a too difficult case on which to test the truth of what I was telling her concerning the mystery of re-birth. All knew, teachers and students alike, that this particular student was incorrigible.

The outer facts of her case were these: The teachers, including the Principal and school Psychiatrist, had sat in judgment on the student just a few days before. They had come to the unanimous decision that the girl, for the good of the school, must be expelled upon reaching her sixteenth birthday. She was rude, crude, unethical and used most vile language. The date for dismissal was but a month away.

As she rode home that night, the teacher kept wondering if she could really change her mind about the girl, and if so, would the student undergo a change of behaviour because she herself had undergone a change of attitude?

The only way to find out would be to try. This would be quite an undertaking for it meant assuming full responsibility for the incarnation of the new values in the student. Did she dare to assume so great a power—such creative, God-like power? This meant a complete reversal of man's normal attitude towards life from "I will love him, if he first loves me", to "He loves me, because I first loved him." This was too much like playing God.

*"We love him, because he first loved us."*

I. JOHN 4:19

But no matter how she tried to argue against it, the feeling persisted that my interpretation gave meaning to the mystery of re-birth by "water and blood".

The teacher decided to accept the challenge. And this is what she did.

She brought the child's face before her mind's eye and saw her smile. She listened and imagined she heard the girl say "Good morning". This was something the student had never done since coming to that school. The teacher imagined the very best about the girl, and then listened and looked as though she heard and saw all that she would hear and see after these things should be. The teacher did this over and over again until she persuaded herself it was true, and fell asleep.

The very next morning, the student entered her classroom and smilingly said, "Good morning". The teacher was so surprised she almost did not respond, and, by her own confession, all through the day she looked for signs of the girl's returning to her former behaviour. However, the girl continued in the transformed state. By the end of the week, the change was noted by all; a second staff meeting was called and the decision of expulsion was revoked. As the child remained friendly and gracious, the teacher has had to ask herself, "Where was the bad child in the first place?"

*"For Mercy, Pity, Peace, and Love Is God, our Father dear,*

*"And Mercy, Pity, Peace, and Love Is man, His child and care."*

"THE DIVINE IMAGE" BLAKE

Transformation is in principle always possible, for the transformed being lives in us, and it is only a question of becoming conscious of it. The teacher had to experience this transformation to know the mystery of "blood and water"; there was no other way, and no man's experience could have been a substitute for her own.

*"We have redemption through his blood."*

EPHESIANS 1:7

Without the decision to change her mind in regard to the child, and the imaginative power to carry it out, the teacher could never have redeemed the student. None can know of the redemptive power of imagination who has not "shed his blood", and tasted the cup of experience.

*"Once read thy own breast right, And thou hast done with fears! Man gets no other light, Search he a thousand years."*

MATTHEW ARNOLD

# 9

# A MYSTICAL VIEW

*"And with many such parables spake he the
word unto them, as they were able to hear it.*

*But without a parable spake he not unto
them: and when they were alone, he
expounded all things to his disciples."*

**MARK 4:33, 34**

This collection of parables which is called the Bible is a revelation of Truth expressed in symbolism to reveal the Laws and
purposes of the Mind of man. As we become aware of deeper
meanings in the parables than those which are usually assigned to
them, we are apprehending them mystically.

For example, let us take a mystical view of the advice given
to the disciples in Matthew 10:10. We read that as the disciples
were ready to teach and practice the great laws of Mind which had
been revealed to them, they were told not to provide shoes for
their journey. A disciple is one who disciplines his Mind that he
may consciously function and act on ever higher and higher levels
of consciousness. The shoe was chosen as a symbol of vicarious

atonement or the spirit of "let-me-do-it-for-you", because the shoe protects its wearer and shields him from impurities *by taking them upon itself*. The aim of the disciple is always to lead himself and others from the bondage of dependency into the liberty of the Sons of God. Hence the advice, *take no shoes*. Accept no intermediary between yourself and God. Turn from all who would offer to do for you what you should, and could, do far better yourself.

> "*Earth's crammed with Heaven, And every common bush afire with God, But only he who sees takes off his shoes.*"
>
> ELIZABETH BARRETT BROWNING

> "*Verily I say unto you, Inasmuch as ye have done it unto one of the least of these my brethren, ye have done it unto me.*"
>
> MATTHEW 25:40

Every time you exercise your imagination on behalf of another, be it good, bad or indifferent, you have literally done that to Christ, for Christ is awakened Human Imagination. Through the wise and loving use of imagination, man clothes and feeds Christ, and through the ignorant and fearful misuse of imagination, man disrobes and scourges Christ.

"Let none of you imagine evil in your hearts against his neighbor" (Zechariah 8:17) is sound but negative advice. A man may stop misusing his imagination on the advice of a friend; he may be negatively served by the experience of others and learn what *not* to imagine, but that is not enough. Such lack of use of the creative power of imagination could never clothe and feed Christ. The purple robe of the Son of God is woven, not by *not* imagining evil, but by imagining the good; by the active, voluntary and loving use of imagination.

> *"Whatsoever things are of good report; if there be any virtue, and if there be any praise, think on these things."*
> PHILIPPIANS 4:8

> *"King Solomon made himself a chariot of the wood of Lebanon. He made the pillars thereof of silver, the bottom thereof of gold, the covering of it of purple, the midst thereof being paved with love . . ."*
> SONG OF SOLOMON 3:9, 10

The first thing we notice is "King Solomon *made himself*". That is what every man must eventually do—*make himself* a chariot of the wood of Lebanon. By chariot, the writer of this allegory means Mind, in which stands the spirit of Wisdom—Solomon—controlling the four functions of Mind that he may build a world of Love and Truth.

"And Joseph made ready his chariot and went up to meet Israel his father." "What tributaries follow him to Rome to grace in captive bonds his chariot wheels?" If man does not make himself a chariot of the wood of Lebanon, then his will be like Queen Mab's: "She is the fairies' midwife; her chariot is an empty hazelnut."

The wood of Lebanon was the mystic's symbol of incorruptibility. To a mystic, it is obvious what King Solomon *made himself*. Silver typified knowledge, gold symbolized wisdom, and purple—a mixture of red and blue—clothed or covered the incorruptible Mind with the red of Love and the blue of Truth.

> *"And they clothed him with purple."*
>
> MARK 15:17

Incarnate, incorruptible four-fold wisdom, clothed in purple—Love and Truth—the purpose of man's experience on earth.

> *Love is the sage's stone;*
> *It takes gold from the clod; It turns naught into aught,*
> *Transforms me into God."*
>
> ANGELUS SILESIUS

# II

# CHARIOT of FIRE: THE IDEAS of NEVILLE GODDARD

By Mitch Horowitz

*This was my first public talk on Neville, delivered June 28, 2013, at the now-defunct arts space Observatory in Gowanus, Brooklyn. It includes the complete talk and the question-and-answer session that followed. —MH*

Some of you know my work, my book *Occult America*, and things that I've done related to that. *Occult America* is a history of supernatural religious movements in our country. A few of you who know my work are aware that I feel strongly that occult, esoteric, and metaphysical movements have touched this country very deeply. I write about these movements not only as a historian who is passionately interested in how the paranormal, occult, and supernatural have influenced our religion, our economy, our psychology, and our views of ourselves; but I also write about these things as a participant, as a kind of a believing historian. I do not view occult thought movements strictly as historical phenomena, which may reveal aspects of human nature; that's true enough, but I think that within the folds of such movements there exist actual ideas for human transformation.

I don't believe in looking into philosophies simply in order to place them in museum cases and to label them. Rather, I think we need practical philosophies that contribute to real-life transformation in the here and now. In my study of different occult and mystical systems, some of which I wrote about in *Occult America* and some of which I'm writing about in my next book *One Simple Idea*, I must tell you the most impactful, elegant, simplest, and dramatically powerful figure I have come across is Neville Goddard.

He was born to an Anglican family on the island of Barbados in 1905. It was a family of ten children, nine boys and one girl. Neville came here to New York City to study theater in 1922. He had some success and also fell into a variety of mystical and occult philosophies. Neville eventually came to feel that he had discovered the master key to existence. Up to this point in my experiments, I conclude: he may have been right.

You can determine that for yourself, because I'm going to start off this presentation by giving you his system. I am also going to provide some history: where he came from, who his teachers were, what his ideas grew out of, who he has influenced, and why he proved vastly ahead of his time. Some of the methods and ideas that Neville experimented with are being heard about today through unsensationalized discussions of developments in quantum physics and neurobiology.

I will also consider the possible identity of the hidden spiritual master named Abdullah who Neville said was his teacher in New York City. Are there spiritual masters, masters of wisdom in the world? Are there beings who can provide help to us when we sincerely desire it? Is that a real possibility or is that just fantasy? I think it's a possibility. It may have played out in his existence.

But we're really here to talk about the practical side of his philosophy. There are many interesting figures who I reference in this talk—dramatic figures whose lives spanned the globe. But we're talking about Neville *because of the usefulness of his ideas* and I want to start with that.

# *Mind as God*

Neville believed very simply in the principle that your imagination is God, the human imagination is God, and that Scripture and all the stories from Scripture, both Old Testament and New Testament, have absolutely no basis in historical reality. The entire book is a metaphor, a blueprint for the individual's personal development. In particular, the New Testament tells the story of God symbolically, of God descending into human form, of humanity becoming asleep to its own divine essence or Christ essence, and believing itself to live within a coarse, limited world of material parameters, of then being crucified and experiencing the agony of his forgetfulness. Christ yells out in the across, "My God, my God, why hast thou forsaken me?" The individual is then resurrected into the realization of his or her divine potentiality, which is the birthright of every individual.

Neville maintained, through his reading of Scripture, his personal probing as a philosopher, and his experiments as an individual, that there is no God outside of the creative powers of the imagination; and that those who wrote Scripture never intended to communicate that there was a God outside of the individual's imagination. The creative force within us—which thinks, plans, pictures, ponders, and falls in and out of emotive states—is symbolically represented in Scripture as God.

Neville maintained that your thoughts, your mental pictures, and your emotive states create your concrete reality—and do at every moment of existence. We are oblivious and asleep to this fact. We live in these coarse shells, we suffer, we cry, we have fleeting joys, we leave these forms. We go through life in a state of slumber without ever knowing that each one of us is a physical form in which creation is experiencing itself. We eventually come to the realization through our causative minds we can experience the powers written about in symbolically in the New Testament and embodied as the story of Christ resurrected.

I want to say to you that Neville meant all of this in the most radical and literal sense. There was nothing inexact or qualified in what he said. He took a radical stand and he continually put up a challenge to his audiences: *try it*. Try it tonight and if it doesn't work, discard me, discard my philosophy, prove me a liar. He sold nothing. He published a handful of books, most of which are now public domain. He gave lectures Grateful Dead-style where he allowed everybody to tape record them and distribute them freely, which is why his talks are now all over the Internet. There's nothing to join. There's nothing to buy. There's no copyright holder. There's just this man and his ideas.

## *Three-Step Miracle*

Neville's outlook can be reduced to a three-part formula, which is incredibly simple, but also requires commitment.

*First*, every creative act begins with an absolute, passionate desire. It sounds so easy, doesn't it? We walk around all day long with desires; I want this, I want that, I want money, I want relationships, I want this person to pay attention to me, I want this attainment. But look again. We often have superficial understandings of our desires and we're dishonest about our desires.

We're dishonest about our desires because we don't want to say to ourselves, in our innermost thoughts, *what we really want*. Sometimes we're repulsed by our desires, and that's the truth. We live in a society that's filled with so much personal license and freedom on the surface, of course, but we often don't want to acknowledge things to ourselves that maybe we believe aren't attractive.

I want to tell a personal story and I want to be very personal with you because I'm talking to you about a man and a philosophy that is enormously challenging and practical, if you really take it seriously. I have no right to be standing here talking to you unless I tell you about some of my own experiences. I want to tell you about one of my personal experiences as it relates to this first point: *desire*. Years ago, I knew a woman who was a psychic. A nationally known person, somebody I assume some of you have heard of, not household name maybe, but well known. I thought she had a genuine psychical gift. I thought she had something.

Yet I didn't like the way she led her life because I thought, personally, that she could be a violent person—not physically violent but emotionally; she would manipulate people around her, bully people, push people around. I didn't really like her but I did feel that she had a true gift. One night I was talking to her. We were on a parking lot somewhere having conversation, and she stopped. She said to me, "You know what you want? You want power. But your problem is that you have an overdeveloped super-ego." As soon as I heard this I wanted to push it away. And I spent years pushing it away. Years pushing it away because I thought to myself, "Well, I don't want power like you. I don't want power to push people around, to bully people, to be violent towards people. I don't want that, no." So I recoiled from what she said. But it haunted me. It haunted me. I could never get away from it.

You don't know really what haunts you until you confront something in yourself, or maybe something that a sensitive person says to you, which leaves the terrible impression that they might just may be speaking the truth. So when Neville talks about desire, he's not talking about something superficial that we keep telling ourselves day after day. He really wants you to get down into the guts of things, where you might want something that makes you very uncomfortable. There are ways we don't like to see ourselves. But Neville maintains that desire is the voice of the God within you; and to walk away from it is to walk away from the potential greatness within yourself. Desire is the language of God. Neville means this in the most literal sense.

*The second step* is physical immobility. This is the part where you actually do something. You enter a physically immobile state. Choose the time of day when you like to meditate, whether it's early morning, whether it's late at night. The time of day Neville chose was 3:00 p.m. He would finish lunch, settle into an easy chair, and go into a drowsy state. Now, this is very important because we think of meditation typically as a state of exquisite awareness. We don't think of meditation as drowsiness. People use these terms in different ways. Neville believed—and as I will talk about this later in this presentation—that the mind is uniquely powerful and suggestible in its drowsy state, hovering just before sleep, but not yet crossing into sleep. It is a controlled reverie. Or a cognizant dream state. Sleep researchers call this hypnagogia. You enter it twice daily: at night when you're drifting off and in the morning when you're coming to (this is sometimes called hypnopompia).

Our minds are exquisitely sensitive at such times. People who suffer from depression or grief describe their early morning hours as the most difficult time of day. The reason for that, I'm convinced, is that it is a time when our rational defenses are down. We're functioning almost entirely from emotion. We are conscious but we are also in this very subtle, fine state between sleep and wakefulness, and our rational defenses are slackened. Let me tell you something vital—and I can attest to this from personal experience. If you are trying to solve a personal problem, do not do it at 5:00 in the morning. Do not.

Your rational defenses are down when you need them most.

When you need your your intellect, whether you're solving a financial problem, whether you're going through a relationship problem, whatever it is, do not use the time of day when it is at its lowest ebb. At 5 a.m. your mind isn't fully working. Your emotions are working. It is a tough, tough time to deal with problems. But it is a very unique time to deal with desires—and for the same reason. When your rational defenses are down, your mind can go in remarkable directions.

I'm going to talk later about developments in psychical research, where there are some extraordinary findings under rigorous clinical conditions, in which people are induced into this hypnagogic state, the state between sleep and wakefulness, and the mind can evince remarkable abilities.

So, Neville said to enter this state of physical immobility. You can most easily do it just before you go to sleep at night. He didn't say do it when you wake up in the morning but I think you can extrapolate that that works, too. You can also do it when you're meditating. You can do it whenever you want. It takes only a few minutes, but go into a very relaxed bodily state or just let yourself be taken into it naturally when you go to bed at night.

And now *the third step*: form a very clear, simple mental scene that would naturally occur following the fulfilment of your desire. Keep it very simple. Run it through your head as long as it feels natural.

A woman attended one of Neville's lectures in Los Angeles and told him simply that she wanted to be married. He told her to enact the mental feeling of a wedding band on her finger. Just that. Keep it very simple. Mentally feel the weight and pressure of the ring on your finger. Maybe feel yourself spinning it around on your finger. Maybe there's something you want from an individual. Select an act that seems simple. Just a handshake, perhaps. Something that communicates that you received something—recognition, a promotion, a congratulation.

You must picture yourself *within* the scene. You must see from within the scene. Don't see yourself doing something as though you're watching it on a screen. Neville was adamant about this. He would say, "If I want to imagine myself climbing a ladder, I don't *see* myself climbing a ladder. *I climb.*" You must feel hands on the ladder. Feel your weight was you step up each rung. You are not watching the scene—you are in it.

Whatever it is, find one simple, clear, persuasive, physical action that would communicate the attainment of your goal, and think from that end, think from the end of the goal fulfilled. Run this through your mind as long as it feels natural.

Neville would always say, "When you open your eyes, you'll be back here in the coarse world that you might not want to be in, but if you persist in this, your assumption will harden into fact." You may wake up, come out of your physical immobility, and discover that the world remains exactly as it was. If you want to be in Paris and you open your eyes in New York, you may be disappointed. Keep doing it and extraordinary events will unfold to secure precisely what you have pictured in your mind. Persistence is key.

## *Using the Emotions*

Now, I want to emphasize one aspect of Neville's philosophy, which I feel that he could have gone further in explaining, and that is the necessity of your visual scene being accompanied by the attendant emotional state. We often make the mistake in the positive-mind movement of equating thought with emotions. They are different things. I have a physical existence. I have intellectual existence. I have an emotional existence. Part of why you may feel torn apart when approaching mind causation is that all of these aspects of your existence—the physical, the mental, and the emotional—are going their own way, running on separate tracks. You may vow not to eat, and you may mean it, but the body wants to eat—and next thing you know the body is in control. You may vow not to get angry—but the emotions take over and you fly into rage. You may think, "I am going to use my intellect and not my passions"—but the passions rule your action. These three forces, body, mind, and intellect, have their own lives—and intellect is the weakest among them. Otherwise we wouldn't struggle with addictions or violent outbursts or impulsive actions. But we find that we are pieces.

This presents a challenge. Because when you enact your mental scene of fulfillment, you also must attain the emotive state that you would feel in your fulfillment. When you approach this teaching you benefit from being a kind of actor or thespian, as Neville was early in his career. Method Acting is a good exercise for enacting this method. Read Stanislavski's *An Actor Prepares*. Anybody who's been trained in Method Acting often learns to use a kind of inner monologue to get themselves into an emotional state. That's a good exercise. You must get the emotions in play.

Let's say you want a promotion at work. You could picture your boss saying to you, "Congratulations—well done!" You must try to feel the emotions that you would feel in that state. Hypnagogia can also help with this because, as noted, the rational defenses are lowered and the mind is more suggestible.

To review Neville's formula: 1) Identify an intense and sincere desire. 2) Enter a state of physical immobility, i.e., the drowsy hypnagogic state. 3) Gently run a scene through your mind that would occur if your wish was fulfilled. Let it be an emotional experience.

# *How It Happened*

I want to tell another personal story. Neville always challenged his listeners: "Test it. Test it. What do you most desire right now? Go home this night and test it. Prove me wrong," he would say. I decided to test him and I want to give you the example. It is recent to this talk, explicit, and absolutely real.

In addition to being a writer, I'm a publisher. I'm the editor-in-chief of a division of Penguin that publishes New Age and metaphysical books. After considerable effort to locate the descendants of the author, I acquired the rights to republish a 1936 self-help book called *Wake Up and Live!* by Dorothea Brande. In this book, Brande writes that the pathology of human nature is what she called a *will to fail*. We fear failure and humiliation more than we crave success, so we constantly sabotage our plans in order to avoid the possibility of failure. We procrastinate. We make excuses. We blow important due dates or wreck professional relationships because we're more frightened of failure than we are hungry for success. But Brande further believed that if you were to *act as though it were impossible to fail*, you could bypass this self-negating pattern and achieve great things.

As mentioned, I spent a year trying to find her descendants so I could buy rights to this book, and I finally did. After this effort, I learned of an audio publisher who wanted to issue out an audio edition. I do a lot of audio narration, although I was still just getting started at this point, and I told this publisher that I was eager to narrate this book. I had recorded for this publisher before. It had been successful and I thought, naturally they'll agree. But they wouldn't get back to me. My e-mails were ignored. My phone calls were ignored. I was very frustrated. I couldn't understand why they wouldn't want me to do this book. I was obviously brimming of passion for it. I had done good work before. But I just couldn't get anywhere. I was totally stuck. I was very frustrated. Finally the publisher replied to me with a decisive, "No."

I thought to myself, "Well, not only do I want to be doing more audiobooks, but this is the kind of book that I was born to read." I went into this exercise and I formed a mental picture. I'm not going to tell you what it was. It was too personal but it was also very simple. I formed a mental picture. I reviewed it faithfully two or three times a day for about two weeks.

Out of the clear blue, without any outer intervention on my part, a rights manager called to say, "Guess what? Someone else actually just bought the rights to that book. It's not with that audio publisher anymore. There's been a change. There's a new audio publisher." I said, "Please tell that new publisher that I am dying to read this book." She got back to me. The new publisher said, "I sent Horowitz an e-mail a week ago asking him to read another audiobook and he never get back to me." I had gotten no such email. I went into my spam folder and found nothing. I went into a still deeper spam filter—and there is was. We signed a deal for me to narrate a total of three books, including *Wake Up and Live!*

I went from being ignored, to being told no, to signing a three-book narration deal. That relationship became one of the most central of my professional life. That same publisher issued this book that you are now reading. I did nothing to influence any of this in the outer world. I didn't do anything or contact anybody. I just did my visualization as Neville prescribed. It ended with the new audio publisher saying, "I contacted him a week ago. Why didn't he get back to me?"

For various reasons, this episode could be considered ordinary and I'm not oblivious to that. But I can say the following: from where I stood, and from long experience, it did not appear ordinary. "Take my challenge and put my words to the test. If the law does not work, its knowledge will not comfort you, and if it is not true, you must discard it. I hope you will be bold enough to test me" That's what Neville said over and over. You don't have to join anything. You don't have to buy anything. You can go online and listen to his lectures. Many of his books can be downloaded for free. His lectures can be downloaded for free. All he would insist is: "Put me to the test. Put me to the test."

## Ecce Homo

Neville was born in 1905 on the island of Barbados, as mentioned. He was not born to a wealthy, land-holding family. He was born to an Anglican family of merchants. He was one of ten children, nine boys and a girl. The family ran a food service and catering business, which later mushroomed into a highly profitable corporation. One of the things that I found about Neville is that the life details and events he claimed in his lectures often turned out to be verifiably true.

I've done a lot of work to track down and verify some of Neville's claims. He came to New York City to study theater and dancing in 1922. He didn't have any money. He was a poor kid and knocked about. He lived in a shared apartment on the Upper West Side on West 75th Street. His large family back home was not rich but over the course of time, they became very rich. They later put him on kind of an allowance or a monthly stipend. Much later, he was able to pursue his studies into the occult, into philosophy, into mysticism, completely independently.

Goddard Industries is today a major catering business in Barbados. They not only cater parties and events, but they cater for airlines. They cater for cruise ships and industrial facilities. By the standards of the West Indies, they're a large and thriving business. Everything that was said in his lectures about his family's growth in fortune is true. His father, Joe or Joseph, founded the business. Neville talks frequently about his older brother Victor, in his lectures. I'm not going to go into all the details here because I have a more exciting example that I want to bring to you, but everything that Neville described about the rise of his family's fortune matches business records and reportage in West Indian newspapers.

Neville lived in Greenwich Village for many years. In the 1940s he was at 32 Washington Square on the west side of Washington Square Park. He spent many years happily there. Now, here was a story that interested me in his lectures and I determined to track down the truth of it. Neville was drafted into the Army on November 12, 1942, just a little less than a year into America's entry to

World War II, so it was at the height of war. Everybody was being drafted. He was a little old to be drafted. He was 37 at that time, but you could still be drafted up to age 45. He tells this story in several of his lectures.

He didn't want to be in the Army. He wanted no part of the war. He wanted to return home to Greenwich Village. At that time, he was married. He had a small daughter, Victoria or Vicky. He had a son from an earlier marriage. He wanted to go back to lecturing. He was in basic training in Louisiana. He asked his commanding officer for a discharge and the commanding officer definitively refused.

So Neville said that every night he would lay down in his cot and imagine himself back home in Greenwich Village, walking around Washington Square Park, back with his wife and family. Every night he'd go to bed in this sensation.

Night after night, he did this for several weeks. And he said that finally, out of the clear blue, the commanding officer came to him and said, "Do you still want to be discharged?" Neville said, "Yes, I do." "You're being honorably discharged," the officer told him.

As I read this, I doubted it. Why would the United States want to discharge a perfectly healthy, athletic male at the height of the America's entry into the Second World War? It made no sense. I started looking for Neville's military records to see if there were other things that would back this up. Neville claimed that he entered the military in late 1942 and then he was honorably discharged about four months later using nothing other than these mental-emotive techniques.

I found Neville's surviving military records. He was, in fact, inducted into the Army on November 12, 1942. I spoke to an Army public affairs spokesman who confirmed that Neville was honorably discharged in March 1943, which is the final record of his U.S. Army pay statement. The reason for the discharge in military records is that he had to return to a "vital civilian occupation." I said to the spokesman, "This man was a metaphysical lecturer, that is not seen as a vital civilian occupation." And he said to me, "Well, unfortunately, the rest of Mr. Goddard's records were destroyed in a fire at a military records facility 1973"—one year following Neville's death.

I know that Neville was back in New York City because *The New Yorker* magazine ran surprisingly extensive profile of him in September of 1943, which places him back on the circuit. He was depicted speaking all around town—in midtown in the Actor's Church, in Greenwich Village, and he completely resumed his career, this "vital civilian occupation" as a metaphysical lecturer. Now, I can't tell you what happened. I can only tell you that the forensics as he described them were accurate. This was one of several instances in which he describes an unlikely story, claims that he used his method as I've described it them you, and, while I can't tell you exactly what happened, I can tell you that the forensics line up.

Neville filled out an application for naturalization and citizenship on September 1, 1943. His address was 32 Washington Square at the time, his age 38 years old. Everything he described in terms of his whereabouts added up.

# *The Source*

I want to say a quick word about where this philosophy came from. Where did Neville get these ideas? His thought was wholly original but everyone has antecedents of some kind. Neville was part of a movement that I call "the positive-thinking movement." Positive-mind metaphysics was a very American philosophy, and it was very much a homegrown philosophy, but, at the same time, every thought that's ever been thought has been encountered by sensitive people in the search extending back to the mythical Hermes, who ancient people in West and Near East considered the progenitor of all ideas and all intellect.

Hermetic philosophy was a Greek-Egyptian philosophy that was written about and set down in the Greek language in the city of Alexandria a few decades following the death of Christ. Neville quotes from one of the Hermetic books in the lecture "Inner Conversations." A central Hermetic theme is that through proper preparation, diet, meditation, and prayer, the individual can be permeated by divine forces. This was a key tenet of Hermeticism. This outlook was reborn during the Renaissance when scholars and translators came to venerate the figure of Hermes Trismegistus, or thrice-greatest Hermes, a Greek term of veneration of Egypt's god of intellect Thoth. Hermes Trismegistus, a mythical man-god, was considered a great figure of antiquity by Renaissance thinkers, of a vintage as old as Moses or Abraham or older still.

Renaissance translators initially believed that the Hermetic literature—tracts that were signed by Hermes Trismegistus, whose name was adopted by Greek-Egyptian scribes—extended back to primeval antiquity. Hermetic writings were considered the source of earliest wisdom. This literature was later correctly dated to late antiquity. After the re-dating, Hermetic ideas eventually fell out of vogue. Some of the intellectual lights of the Renaissance had placed great hopes that the writings attributed to Hermes Trismegistus possessed great antiquity. And when those hopes of antiquity were and these writings were accurately dated to late antiquity, the readjustment of the timeline, I think tragically for Western civilization, convinced many people that the whole project of the Hermetic literature was somehow compromised. For that reason there are, to this day, relatively few quality translations of the Hermetic literature. The dating issue assumed too great a proportion in people's minds. The fact is, all ancient literature, just like all religions, are built from earlier ideas, and I believe the Hermetic philosophy was a retention of much older oral philosophy. Most scholars today agree with that.

In any case, the Hermetic ideas faded. Including the core principle that the human form could be permeated by something higher and could itself attain a kind of creative and clairvoyant power. These ideas that were so arousing, that created such hope and intrigue during Renaissance, got pushed to the margins. But they eventually reentered the public mind in part through the influence of Franz Anton Mesmer (1734–1815), who was a lawyer and a self-styled physician of Viennese descent. Mesmer appeared in Paris in 1778, in the decade preceding the French Revolution. He entered into royal courts with this radical theory that all of life was animated by this invisible etheric fluid which he called *animal magnetism.*

Mesmer maintained that if you place an individual into a kind of trance state, what we would call a hypnotic trance—recall Neville talking about this state of drowsiness, this hypnagogic state—you could then realign his or her animal magnetism, this ethereal life fluid, and cure physical or mental diseases, and, according to practitioners, introduce powers such as clairvoyance or the ability to speak in unknown foreign tongues. You could heal. You could empower. You could get at the life stuff of the individual. I was recently in a Walgreen's drugstore and saw an ad reading, "Mysterious and Mesmerizing," for a skin lotion. It's funny how occult language, unmoored from its meaning, lingers in daily life.

Mesmer was feted in royal courts but his philosophy aroused suspicion. At the instigation of King Louis XVI, Mesmerism was discredited by a royal commission in 1784. This investigatory commission was chaired by Benjamin Franklin, who at the time was America's ambassador to France. The commission concluded that there was no such thing as animal magnetism and that whatever cures or effects were experienced under the influence of a mesmeric trance were "in the imagination." But there the committee left dangling its most extraordinary question. If it's "in the imagination," why should there be any effects at all?

Mesmer's greatest students edged away from the idea of animal magnetism as some physical, ethereal fluid. They believed something else was at work. In their struggle for answers, they arrived at the first descriptions of what we would later call subliminal mind and then the subconscious or unconscious mind. Mesmer's proteges did not possess a psychological vocabulary—they preceded and in some regards prefigured modern psychology—but they knew that *something* was evident and effective in his theory of animal magnetism. The best students morphed the master's theories into an early, rough iteration of the subconscious mind. This is an overlooked and crucial basis for the growth of modern psychology. The terms subliminal and subconscious mind began to be heard in the 1890s.

Mesmer died in 1815. But his ideas were taken up in many quarters including, fatefully, by a New England clockmaker named Phineas Quimby (1802–1866). Starting in the late 1830s, Quimby began to experiment with how states of *personal excitement* could make him feel better physically. Quimby suffered from tuberculosis and he discovered that when he would take vigorous carriage rides in the Maine countryside, the effects of tuberculosis would lift. Quimby began to probe the state of his mood and the state of his physical wellbeing. He treated others and became known as a mental healer in the mid-1840s.

At first, Quimby worked with a teenaged boy named Lucius Burkmar. Lucius would enter a trance or hypnagogic state from which he was said to be able to clairvoyantly view people's bodily organs and diagnose and prescribe cures for diseases. Quimby discovered that sometimes the cures that Lucius prescribed, which were often botanical remedies or herbal teas, had previously been prescribed by physicians—and did not work. But when Lucius prescribed them, *they often did work.* The difference, Quimby concluded, was in the *confidence of the patient.* Quimby stopped working with Lucius and encouraged patients to arouse mental energies on their own.

American medicine in the mid-1840s was in a horrendously underdeveloped state. It was the one area of the sciences in which American lagged behind Europe. People had some reason to be driven to mental healers and prayer healers because, if anything, they were less dangerous than most of what was then standard allopathic medicine, which involved measures that were medieval. Physicians were performing bloodletting, administering mercury and other poisons and narcotics. At the very least, the mental healing movement caused no harm.

And, according to historical letters, articles, and diaries, sometimes it did a lot of good. Someone who briefly served as a student to Quimby was Mary Baker Eddy (1821–1910), who founded her own movement called Christian Science. Eddy taught that the healing ministry of Christ is an ever-present fact that is still going on on Earth, and that individuals could be healed by the realization that there is only one true reality and that is this great divine mind that created the universe and that animates everything around us; and further that matter, these forms that we live in, and the floorboards underneath our feet, are not real. They are illusory, as are illness, prejudice, violence, and all human corruption. Eddy taught that through prayer and proper understanding of Scripture, the individual could be healed. She was a remarkable figure. Sometimes people will say, in a far too hasty way, "Well, she took all her ideas from Quimby." It's not that simple. Her interlude with Quimby in the early 1860s was vitally important in her development; but her ideas were uniquely her own. She was an extraordinary figure. I don't think we've taken full measure in this culture of how influential Mary Baker Eddy's ideas have been.

Another figure who become indirectly influential in this healing movement was Emanuel Swedenborg (1688–1772), a Swedish scientist and mystic who worked primarily in the 1700s. Swedenborg's central idea was that the mind is a conduit, a capillary, of cosmic laws, and everything that occurs in the world, including our own thoughts, mirrors events in an invisible world, a spiritual world, which we do not see but always interact with. Everything that men and women do on Earth, Swedenborg taught, is a reflection of something occurring in this unseen world, and our minds are almost like receiving stations, spiritual telegraphs, for messages and ideas from a cosmic plane in which we cannot directly participate but are vitally linked.

Swedenborg was an influence on a Methodist minister named Warren Felt Evans, who was also a contemporary of Quimby's, and who briefly worked with him. Evans wrote a book in 1869 called *The Mental Cure* which was the first book to use the term "new age" in the spiritual sense that it's used today. Evans believed that through prayer, proper direction of thought, use of affirmations, and assumption of a confident mental state, the individual could be cured. *The Mental Cure* is not read anywhere today. Yet it is a surprisingly sprightly book. You'd be surprised. When I first had to read *The Mental Cure* I braced myself but I found that its pages turn quite effortlessly. Evans was a brilliant writer. All of his books are obscure today. But he was a seminal figure in the creation of a positive-thinking movement.

More indirectly, the British poet William Blake also had a certain influence on this movement, and on Neville in particular. Blake believed that humans dwell in this coarse world where we are imprisoned in a fortress of illusions; but the one true mind, the great creative imagination of God, can course through us. We can "cleanse the doors of perception." We can feel the coursing of this great mind within us.

These are some of the same ideas that resounded in Hermeticism. There wasn't a direct connection, necessarily. First of all, there weren't many translations of some of the Hermetic literature, which a man like Blake could likely draw upon. People from different epochs and eras often arrived at these parallel cosmic ideas themselves. When academic writers approach New Thought or the positive-thinking movement, they sometimes make the mistake of conflating it with the idealist philosophy of figures like Berkeley, Kant, Hegel, and later Schopenhauer and Nietzsche. The positive-thinking figures were not directly influenced by the idealists. Those figures and their phraseology are absent in early positive-mind writings. People sometimes make the mistake of not realizing that in a country like America, which was a very agricultural country throughout most of the 19th century, little of this material was directly available.

As an example, consider the Tao Te Ching. This great ancient Chinese work on ethics and philosophy wasn't even translated into English until 1838. In the mid-1840s, there existed four

English-language copies in all of the United States. One was in the library at Harvard, one was in Ralph Waldo Emerson's library which he lent out, and two were in private hands. It wasn't like somebody like Phineas Quimby, the New England clockmaker, who was experimenting with moods and the body, could locate Taoist or Hermetic philosophy, or could even read translations of Hegel. Literacy aside, many of these things weren't accessible. It's a mistake to conclude that because one system of thought mirrors another, that the preceding system is necessarily the birth mother of the later one. In the rural environs of America, many of the positive-mind theorists were independently coming up with these ideas.

Moving into the 20th century, we encounter a figure who directly influenced Neville—French mind theorist Emile Coué (1857–1926). Coué was a largely self-trained hypnotherapist. He died in 1926, but shortly before he died, he made two lecture tours of the United States. Coué was hugely popular in the US and in England. He had a key theory, which rested on the principle that when you enter a sleepy drowsy state, the hypnagogic state, your mind is uniquely supple, suggestible, and powerful. Coué came up with a method to use in conjunction with this state. His system was so simple that critics mocked it. You've probably heard of it. Coué told people to gently repeat the mantra, "Day by day, in every way, I am getting better and better." He said you should lay in bed and recite this just as you're drifting off at night and again just as you're coming to in the morning. Whisper it twenty times to yourself. You could knot a piece of string twenty times and take that piece of string with you, keep it at your bedside, so you could count off your repetitions like a rosary.

Coué had many thousands of followers, but he also became a figure of ridicule because the critics said: "How could such a simple idea possibly do anything for anyone?" Of course, they would not try it. To their minds, it was prima facie nonsense. Such an attitude reminds me of the character of Dr. Zaius from *Planet of the Apes* insisting that flight is a physical impossibility. Thought in the absence of experience is the impoverishment of our intellectual culture. Certainty in the absence of personal experience precludes effort.

In addition to the uses of hypnagogia, another of Coué's ideas appeared in Neville's thought system. You can find the language from time to time in Neville's lectures and writing. That is, within human beings exist two forces: *will* and *imagination*. The *will* is intellectual self-determination. The *imagination* is the mental images and emotionally conditioned reactions that populate our psyches, particularly with regard to self-image. Coué said that when imagination and will are in conflict, *imagination always win*. Your emotional state always overcomes your intellect.

As an example, Coué said, place a wooden plank on the floor and ask an average person to walk across it. He or she will have no problem. But if you raise that same wooden plank twenty feet off the ground, in many cases the person will be petrified even though there's no difference in the physical demand. They are capable of walking across it. The risk of falling is minimal. *The change in condition alone creates an emotional state that makes them more nervous and hence accident prone.* Coué believed it necessary to cultivate new imaginative images of ourselves. We cannot do that through the intellect alone. But we can do so by making using of this very subtle hypnagogic state. He called his method auto-suggestion. It was self-hypnosis essentially. Neville adopted the method, if not the same assumptions behind it.

## The Mystic in Life

There are few pictures of Neville. His smiles glowingly in rare pictures toward the end of his life. He died young at age 67 in 1972. He died of heart failure in West Hollywood where he was living with his family. Until the end, his voice and his powers of communication never left him. They absolutely resonated.

It's interesting sometimes to look at the lives of mystical figures like Neville who are hard to pin down, but who did lead domestic lives. There was a little piece in the *Los Angeles Times* on October 21, 1962: "Ms. Goddard Named as College President." It went on, "Miss Victoria Goddard, daughter of Mr. and Mrs. Neville Goddard, has been appointed co-chairman of campus publicity by the student government president at Russell Sage College for New York. She is an English major." This was Neville's daughter.

Now, Victoria Goddard or Vicky as she's known, is still living. She lives in Los Angeles in the family house that she once resided in with her parents. She avoids publicity and contact with people who are interested in Neville's ideas. I've tried to reach out to her but she has no interest in being in touch. She did give her approval indirectly to an anthology of Neville's writings that I wrote an introduction to, but she doesn't want contact with his students. She wants to lead her own existence. But it's funny sometimes we come across little things like this article or a photograph and realize that every one of us share the same workaday concerns.

For all of Neville's wonderful mystical theories, I just have to share this little discourse that he went into about Liquid-Plumr in a lecture that he delivered in 1970. I found this a delightful reminder of how the ordinary steps into all of our lives even when we're trying to deal with cosmic and mystical concerns. He told an audience in 1970:

So you buy something because of highly publicized TV promotions. Someone highly publicized what is called "Liquid-Plumr." And so I had some moment in my bathroom where the sink was all stopped up, so I got the Liquid-Plumr. Poured it in, in abundance. It said it's heavier than water, and it would go all the way down and just eat up everything that is organic and will not hurt anything that is not organic, so I poured it in. Water still remained; it didn't go down. Called the plumber the next day. He couldn't come that day but he would come the next day. So it was forty-eight hours. So when he came the entire sink was eaten away by the Liquid-Plumr. So I asked him: "Does this thing work?" He said: "It does for two people: the one who manufactures it, and the one who sells it." They are the only ones who profit by the Liquid-Plumr. And so you turned on the TV and you saw it and you bought it. It is still on TV and I am sinning, because to sin by silence when I should protest makes cowards of us all. But I haven't protested to the station that advertises this nonsense and I haven't protested to the place where I got it or to anyone who manufactures it, so I am the silent sinner. Multiply me because of my embarrassment. Here is a sink completely eaten up by Liquid-Plumr.

"The silent sinner," he called himself. I lodge letters of protest and phone calls from time to time, so I can sympathize with everything Neville says here.

Neville published a variety of books during his lifetime, most of them quite short. There was a company in Los Angeles called G and J Publishing which issued most of his books. A symbol appeared on most of his covers, which he devised himself. It was a heart with an eye to symbolize eternal vision, inner vision, and it was part of a fruit-bearing tree. As the emotive state of man conceives, so the tree brings forth fruit.

In 1964, Neville published an extremely rare pamphlet called, *He Breaks The Shell*. On its cover you can see a little cherub or angelic figure coming out of a human head. Neville described this mystical experience and said that this is an experience that all of us will have either in this lifetime or another; and that the whole purpose of human existence is to be reborn from your imagination; and your imagination, as we experience it, is physically lodged in your skull, entombed in this kind of a womb. Christ was crucified in Golgotha, place of the skull. Neville believed that we each will be reborn from within our own skull, and that we will have an actual physical experience, maybe in the form of a dream, but a vivid, tactile experience of being reborn from out of the base of our skull. We will know, in that moment, that we are fulfilling our essential purpose.

He described this quite vividly. He had this experience in New York City in 1959 where he had an enormously tactile, sensationally real dream of being reborn from out of the skull. Minerva was said to have been reborn from the skull of Zeus or Jupiter. Christ was crucified at the place of the skull. "You and I," Neville said, "will be reborn from within our skull." In the late 1960s a booking agent told him, "Listen, you've got to stop telling this story at your talks. It's freaking everyone out. People want to hear the get-rich stuff." He told Neville that he if did not change course he'd have no audience left. "Then I'll tell it to the bare walls," Neville replied. He spoke of his mystical experience for the rest of his career until he died in 1972.

I reissued one of Neville's books recently, *The Power of Awareness*. I felt that, for the first time, Neville's books needed to be packaged in a way that fits their dignity, and this is a beautiful edition that I took great joy in working on because I thought it represented him with the right degree of dignity.

I want to quote from Neville's voice. He spoke in such beautiful, resonant language, so unhaltingly, never a pause, never an uncertainty. He knew his outlook so well, he could share it effortlessly. Here is his voice.

> So I'm telling you of the power within you and that power is your own wonderful human imagination. And that is the only God in the world. There is no other God. That is the Jesus Christ of Scripture, so tonight take it seriously. If you really have an objective in this world and you're waiting for something to happen on the outside to make it so, forget it. Do it in your own wonderful human imagination. Actually bring it into being in your own imagination. Conjure a scene which would imply the fulfillment of that dream and lose yourself in the action as you contemplate it, and completely lose yourself in that state. If you're completely absorbed in it, you will objectify it and you will see it seemingly independent of your perception of it. But even if you do not have that intensity, if you lose yourself in it and feel it to true—the imaginal act—then drop it. In a way you do not know, it will become true.

If you are interested in hearing more of Neville, you can go online and find lectures that are posted on YouTube and almost everywhere. He allowed people who came to presentations to tape record them and freely distribute them. He claimed copyright over nothing, and that, to me, is the mark of a real leader. That's the mark of a real thinker. You don't have to join anything. You don't have to ask anybody permission for anything. You don't have to pay any dues. You don't have to buy anything. You just start.

# Neville's Circle

I want to say a quick word about some of the people who have been influenced by Neville today. One of them is the major-league baseball pitcher, Barry Zito, who actually introduced me to Neville. I was doing an article about Barry in 2003 and he said to me, "Oh, you must be into Neville," and I said, "I've never heard of him." He said, "Really? You never heard of him?" He was the first one who got me interested in Neville's thought, and that was a huge influence in my life. It was almost 10 years ago to this very day and in many regards put me where I am today.

The New Age writer Wayne Dyer wrote a lot about Neville in his most recent book which is called *Wishes Fulfilled*. But a really remarkable influence that Neville brought into the world came in the form his subtle impact on the writer, Carlos Castaneda, of whom I'm a great admirer. I want to read a short passage from my forthcoming book, *One Simple Idea*:

By the mid-1950s, Neville's life story exerted a powerful pull on a budding writer whose own memoirs of mystic discovery later made him a near-household name: Carlos Castaneda. Castaneda told his own tales of tutelage under a mysterious instructor, in his case a Native American sorcerer named Don Juan. Castaneda first discovered Neville through an early love interest in Los Angeles, Margaret Runyan, who was among Neville's most dedicated students. A cousin of American storyteller Damon Runyon, Margaret wooed the stocky Latin art student at a friend's house, slipping Carlos a slender Neville volume called *The Search,* in which she had inscribed her name and phone number. The two became lovers and later husband and wife. Runyan spoke frequently to Castaneda about her mystical teacher Neville, but he responded with little more than mild interest—with one exception.

In her memoirs, Runyan recalled Castaneda growing fascinated when the conversation turned to Neville's discipleship under an exotic teacher. She wrote:

It was more than the message that attracted Carlos, it was Neville himself. He was so mysterious. Nobody was really sure who he was or where he had come from. There were vague references to Barbados in the West Indies and his being the son of an ultra-rich plantation family, but nobody knew for sure. They couldn't even be sure about this Abdullah business, his Indian teacher, who was always way back there in the jungle, or someplace. The only thing you really knew was that Neville was here and that he might be back next week, but then again . . .

"There was," Runyon concluded, "a certain power in that position, an appealing kind of freedom in the lack of past and Carlos knew it."

*Carlos knew it.* Both Neville and Castaneda were dealing the same basic idea, and one that has a certain pedigree in America's alternative spiritual culture: tutelage under hidden spiritual masters.

Neville again and again told this story, that there was a turbaned black man of Jewish descent who tutored him starting in 1931 in kabbalah, Scripture, number symbolism, and mental metaphysics. He described Abdullah as this somewhat taciturn, mysterious figure who he met one day at a metaphysical lecture in 1931. Neville walked in and Abdullah said to him, "Neville, you're six months late." Neville said, "I had never seen this man before." Abdullah continued, "The brothers told me you were coming and you're six months late." He said they spent the next five years together studying.

Neville had his first true awakening experience in the winter of 1933. He was dying to get out of the Manhattan winter. He wanted to spend Christmas back home with his family in Barbados. He had no money and Abdullah said to him, "Walk the streets of Manhattan as if you are there and you shall be." And so Neville said he would walk the gray wintry streets of the Upper West Side with the feeling that he was in the palm-lined lanes of Barbados. He would go to see Abdullah, telling him, "It isn't working. I'm still here." And Abdullah would slam the door in his face and say, "You're not here. You're in Barbados."

Then one day, before the last ship departed for Barbados, his brother, Victor, from out of the blue, without any physical intercession on Neville's part, sent him a first-class steamer ticket and $50. "Come spend winter with us in Barbados," he wrote. Neville said he was transformed by the experience. He felt that it was Abdullah's law of mental assumption came to his rescue.

Now, this idea of mysterious spiritual masters got popularized in modern Western culture through the influence of Madame Blavatsky and her partner Colonel Henry Steel Olcott who founded the movement of Theosophy in New York City in 1975. They claimed to be under the tutelage of hidden spiritual masters, Master Koot Hoomi, who was said to be Tibetan, and Master Morya who was said to be Indian. These adepts, they said, would send them phenomenally produced letters, advising them what to do, giving them directions, giving them advice, giving them succor. Around that time, Colonel Olcott and Madame Blavatsky were living in a building which is still standing at the corner of 8th Avenue of West 47th Street which was known as the Lamasery, their headquarters or salon, where they dwelt on the second floor. Today it is an Econo Lodge. None of the people who worked there were very entranced with my attempts to explain the history of the building.

Colonel Olcott said that one time in the winter of 1877, Master Morya materialized in his room and directed him and Madame Blavatsky to relocate to the nation of India, which they did the following year. They helped instigate the Indian independence movement. Olcott went on speaking tours all over the Near East, Far

East, Japan, Sri Lanka. He helped instigate a rebirth of Buddhism throughout the East. Blavatsky and Olcott were enormously effective in their way. Colonel Olcott attributed all of it to the presence of these mysterious spiritual masters, these great turbaned figures somewhere from the East who had given them instruction.

Now, I first wrote about Neville in an article that was published in February 2005 in *Science of Mind* magazine called "Searching for Neville Goddard." Things had been fairly quiet around Neville for many years, and that article attracted a lot of interest. I started receiving phone calls and e-mail after e-mail asking me, who was Abdullah? Did he exist? Could he be identified? I would tell people at the time that I thought Abdullah was a kind of a mythos that Neville might have borrowed, clipped and pasted, from Theosophy. I didn't think there was any evidence to show that Abdullah was a real person, and I thought the dramatic claims around him were probably Neville's mythmaking.

Now, to my surprise, I discovered something about Abdullah through another figure in the positive thinking movement, a man named Joseph Murphy, who died in 1981, and who wrote a very popular book, which some of you may have read, called *The Power of Your Subconscious Mind*. Shortly before his death, Murphy gave a series of interviews to a French-speaking minister from Quebec. The interviewer published his book only in French with Quebec press. It is called *Dialogues with Joseph Murphy* and in these interviews Murphy offhandedly remarks that he, too, was a student of Abdullah. Murphy actually came to New York around the same time as Neville in 1922. He migrated from Ireland. Murphy worked as a pharmacist at the Algonquin Hotel. They used to have a little pharmacy in their lobby. And Murphy also became a metaphysical lecturer and was acquainted with Neville for several years. He stated very simply and matter-of-factly that Abdullah was his teacher too, and that he was a very real man.

I began to look around and correspond with people, and I came to feel, over the past few years, that I happened upon a figure who might actually be Abdullah. He was Arnold Josiah Ford. Ford was a mystic, black nationalist, and part of a movement called the Black Hebrew Movement which still exists in various forms. Ford was born in Barbados, Neville's home island, in 1877. Ford emigrated to Harlem in 1910. He became involved with Marcus Garvey's Universal Negro Improvement Association, of which he was musical director. In surviving photographs Ford, like Abdullah, is turbaned.

In addition to being a dedicated follower of Marcus Garvey—who had his own mind-power metaphysics, about which I'll say a quick word in a moment—Ford was also part of a movement called Ethiopianism. It was a precursor to Rastafarianism. Ford believed, as the Rastafarian people do, as many other people do with good reason, that Ethiopia, one of the oldest continuous civilizations on Earth and one of the most populous nations in Africa, was home to a lost tribe of Israel, which, in this line of teaching, had its own blend of what we know as traditional historical Judaism and mystical teachings and mental metaphysics.

The movement of Ethiopianism believed that this lost African-Israelite tribe harbored a great wealth of ancient teachings that had been lost to most modern people. The Ethiopianism movement believed in mind-power metaphysics and mental healing. Ford was considered a rabbi and he had his own African-American congregation in Harlem. He described himself a man of authentic Israelite and Jewish descent. Writing in 1946, occult philosopher Israel Regardie described Neville's Abdullah as an "Ethiopian rabbi." Regardie, who had been a secretary to the occultist, Aleister Crowley, is quoted on Neville in the introduction.

According to census records, Ford was living in Harlem 1931. He identified his occupation to the census taker as rabbi. That was the same year that Neville met Abdullah. (Although he later gave Abdullah's address as the Upper West Side, not Harlem.) Neville may have been playing around with the name a little bit. He would affectionately refer to Abdullah in his lectures as *Ab*. Ab is a variant of the Hebrew word *abba* for father. Perhaps he saw Abdullah, Ford, as kind of a father figure. He said they studied metaphysics, Scripture, Kabbalah together for five years. Ford has been written about in histories of the Black Hebrew Movement as a key figure who brought authentic knowledge of the Hebrew language, Talmud, and Kabbalah into the Black Hebrew Movement as it existed in Harlem at that time.

Ford was a person of some learning. He was, as I said, a follower of Marcus Garvey, a figure about whom I write in *Occult America*. Garvey has not been properly understood in our culture. He was a pioneering black nationalist figure. He was a great pioneering activist and voice of liberation. He was also very much into his own brand of mental metaphysics. You might recognize this statement of Garvey's which Bob Marley adapted in the lyrics to *Redemption Song:* "We are going to emancipate ourselves from mental slavery because whilst others might free the body, none but ourselves can free the mind." Garvey's speeches are shot through with New Thought language, with the language of mental metaphysics. This was an essential part of Garvey's outlook. This perspective was also essential to the culture of Ethiopianism, which saw Ethiopia's crowned emperor, Haile Selassie, who was coronated in 1930, as a messianic figure. The movement of Ethiopianism morphed into Rastafarianism. It started in the mid-1930s.

Now, there are a lot of correspondences between Arnold Josiah Ford and Neville's description of Abdullah, including physical correspondences, the turban and such. But for all that I've noted, the timeline does not match up sufficiently to make any of this conclusive; because Ford left America sometime in 1931, and he moved to the Ethiopian countryside. After Haile Selassie was coronated as emperor, he offered a land grant to any African-American willing to emigrate to Ethiopia. The emperor saw Ethiopia in a way that matched Ford's ideals as a kind of African-Israel. Haile Selassie wanted Afro-Caribbean and Afro-American people to move, or to come home as he saw it, to Ethiopia, so he offered land grants.

Ford and about thirty followers of Ethiopianism in New York accepted the land grants. There's been some debate about when Ford left, but I have a *New York Times* article that places Ford in New York City still in December 1930. He didn't leave until 1931. That was the same year that Neville said they met. The timeline doesn't match up because Neville said they studied together for five years, so it's possible that Ford was one of several teachers that Neville had, and he created a kind of composite figure who he called Abdullah, Ab, father, of whom Ford may have been a part.

Now, in a coda to Ford's life, I must take note that it was a tougher and braver and more brutal existence back then in some regards. Ford, who for 20 years has been living as a musician and a rabbi in Harlem, moved to rural Ethiopia, the northern part of this nation, to accept Haile Selassie's land grant. He died there in 1935. Tragically, there are no records of Ford's life in Ethiopia. It must have been very difficult. Imagine being a metropolitan person and uprooting yourself to a completely rural setting in a developing nation in the 1930s, and Mussolini is beating the war drum, and Mussolini's fascist troops invaded Ethiopia just weeks after Ford's death, across the north border. This was a man who put himself through tremendous ordeals for his principles. I cannot conclude that Ford was Abdullah. But Murphy's testimony suggests that there *was* an Abdullah, and I think Ford corresponds in many ways—and I write about this in *One Simple Idea*; there probably is some intersection there.

There's another figure I want to mention of a very different kind whose thought had some indirect intersection with Neville's, and that is Aleister Crowley, the British occultist. Crowley made a very interesting statement in a book that he received in a way that we might call channeled perception in 1904; it was later published broadly in 1938 called *The Book of the Law*. In his introduction, Crowley writes:

Each of us has thus an universe of his own, but it is the same universe for each one as soon as it includes all possible experience. This implies the extension of consciousness to include all other consciousnesses. In our present stage, the object that you see is never the same as the one that I see; we infer that it is the same because your experience tallies with mine on so many points that the actual differences of our observation are negligible . . . Yet all the time neither of us can know anything . . . at all beyond the total impression made on our respective minds.

Neville said something similar:

Do you realize that no two people live in the same world? We may be together now in this room, but we will go home tonight and close our doors on entirely different worlds. Tomorrow, we will go to work where we'll meet others but each one of us lives in our own mental and physical world.

Neville meant this in the most literal sense. He believed that every individual, possessed of his or her own imagination, is God, and that everyone you see, including me standing in this room, is rooted in you, as you are ultimately rooted in God.

You exist in this world of infinite possibilities and realities, and that, in fact, when you mentally picture something, you're not creating it—it already exists. You're claiming it. The very fact of being able to experience it mentally confirms that in this world of infinite possibilities, where imagination is the ultimate creative agent, everything that you can picture *already is.*

# Mind Science

Some of the things that Neville said prefigured studies both in psychical research and quantum physics. I want to say a quick word about that. One of my heroes is, J.B. Rhine, a psychical researcher who performed tens of thousands of trials at Duke University in the 1930s and beyond to test for clairvoyant perception. Rhine often used a five-suit deck of cards called Zener cards; if you were guessing a card, you had a one-in-five chance, 20 percent, of naming the right card. As Rhine documented in literally tens of thousands of trials, with meticulous clinical control, certain individuals persistently, under controlled conditions, scored higher than a chance hit of 20 percent.

It wasn't always dramatically higher. It wasn't like Zeus was aiming lightning bolts at the Earth. But if someone over the course of thousands of trials keeps scoring 25 percent, 26 percent, 27 percent, beyond all chance possibility, and the results are parsed, juried, gone over, reviewed, you have some anomalous transfer of information going on in a laboratory setting. Rhine's research was real. And Rhine noticed—and he had this quietly monumental way of describing things, he would make some observation in a footnote that could be extraordinary—that the correlation to a high success rate of hits on the Zener cards was usually a feeling of enthusiasm, positive expectation, hopefulness, belief in the possibility of ESP, and an encouraging environment. Then when boredom or physical exhaustion would set in, or interest would wane, the results would go down. If interest was somehow renewed, revised, if there was a feeling of comity in the testing room, the results would go up.

We as a culture haven't begun to deal with the implications of Rhine's experiments. There was another parapsychologist, Charles Honorton, who began a series of experiments in 1970s—I see him as Rhine's successor—called the *ganzfeld* experiments. Ganzfeld is German for whole field. Honorton experimented on subjects who were in a hypnagogic state, the state of drowsiness. Honorton and his collaborators theorized that if you could induce the near-sleep state in an individual, put somebody in conditions of comfortable isolation, fit them with eye coverings and headphones emitting white noise or some kind of negative sound to listen to, put them in a greatly relaxed state, it might be possible to heighten the appearance of some kind of clairvoyant faculty.

His test was to place a subject, a receiver, into a comfortable isolation tank, and to place another subject, a sender, in a different room. Then the sender attempted to mentally convey an image—such as a flower, a rocket, a boat, or something else—to the receiver, and see what happens. These tests generally used four images. Three were decoys, one was actual. Again, in certain subjects, and also in the subjects as a whole in the form of meta-analysis, Honorton found over and over again results that showed a higher than 25 percent chance hit when subjects were placed into the hypnagogic state.

We're in this state all the time. When you're napping, when you're dozing off at your desk, when you're going to sleep at night, when you're waking up in the morning. Neville's message is: *use it.* Honorton died very young in 1992 at age 46. He had suffered health problems his whole life. If he had lived, his name would, I believe, be as well-known as J.B. Rhine. He was a great parapsychologist.

There's another field burgeoning today called neuroplasticity that relates to some of Neville's sights. In short, brain imaging shows that repeat thoughts change the pathways through which electrical impulses travel in your brain. This has been used to treat obsessive compulsive disorder. A research psychologist named Jeffery Schwartz at UCLA has devised a program that ameliorates and dissipates obsessive thoughts. Schwartz's program teaches patients and people in his clinical trials to substitute something in place of an obsessive thought at the very moment they experience it. This diversion may be a pleasurable physical activity, listening to music, jogging, whatever they want, just anything that gets them off that obsessive thought. Schwartz has found through brain imaging, and many scientists have replicated this data, that if you repeat an exercise like that, eventually biologic changes manifest in the brain, neuropathways change, thoughts themselves alter brain biology as far as electrical impulses are concerned.

A New Thought writer in 1911, who theorized without any of the contemporary brain imaging and neuroscience, came up with exactly the same prescription. His name was John Henry Randall. Randall called it *substitution.* His language and the language used today by 21st century researchers in neuroplasticity is extraordinarily similar.

Finally, we have emerging from the field of quantum physics an extraordinary set of questions, which have been coming at us actually for 80-plus years, about the extent to which observation influences the manifestation of subatomic particles. I want to give a very brief example. Basically, quantum physics experiments have shown that if you direct a wave of particles, often in the form of a light wave, at a target system, perhaps a double-slit box or two boxes, the wave of light will collapse into a particle state, it will go from a wave state to a particle state. This occurs when a conscious observer is present or a measurement is occurring. Interference patterns demonstrate that the particle-like properties of wave of light *at one time appeared in both boxes*. Only when someone decided to look or to take a measurement did the particles become localized in one box.

In 1935, physicist Erwin Schrodinger noted that the conclusions of these quantum experiments were so outrageous, were so contrary to all observed experience, that he devised a thought experiment called Schrodinger's Cat in order to highlight this surreality. Schrodinger did not intend his thought experiment to endorse quantum theorizing. He intended it to compel quantum theorists to deal with the ultimate and, what he considered, absurdist conclusions of their theories—theories which have never been overturned, theories which have been affirmed for 80 years. Now, Schrodinger's Cat comes down to this, it can be put this way: You take two boxes. You put a cat into one of the two boxes. You direct a subatomic particle at the boxes. One box is empty, one box holds the cat. Inside the box with the cat is what he called a "diabolical device." This diabolical device trips a beaker of poison when it comes in contact with a subatomic particle, thus killing the cat.

So, you do your experiment. You direct the particle and you go to check the boxes. Which box is the particle in? Is the cat dead? Is the cat alive? The cat is *both*, Schrodinger insisted. It must be *both* because the subatomic particle can be shown to exist in more than one place, in a wave state, until someone checks, and thus localizes it into a particle state, occupying one place. Hence, you must allow for both outcomes—you have a dead/alive cat. That makes no sense. All of lived experience says that you've got two boxes; you've got one cat; the cat's dead if you fired into the box with the cat; or the cat's alive if you fired into the other box. Schrodinger said, "Not so." Interference experiments demonstrate that at one point the subatomic particle was in a *wave state*; it was non-local; it existed only in potential; it existed in both boxes and, given the nature of quantum observation, potentially everywhere. It is only when you go to check and open one of the boxes that the particle becomes localized. *It was in both boxes until a conscious observer made the decision to check.*

A later group of physicists argued there's no doubting Schrodinger's conclusion, and in fact, if you were to check eight hours later, you would not only find a cat that was living/dead, but you would find a living cat that was hungry because it hadn't been fed for eight hours. The timing itself created a past, present, and future for the cat—a reality selected out of infinite possibilities. Schrodinger didn't intend for his thought experiment to affirm this radical departure from reality. He intended it to expose what he considered the absurdist conclusions of quantum physics. But quantum physics data kept mounting and mounting, and Schrodinger's thought experiment became to some physicists a very real illustration of the extraordinary physical impossibilities that we were seeing in the world of quantum physics.

*The implication is that we live in a serial universe—that there are infinite realities, whether we experience them or not; and our experience of one of these realties rests on observation.* If we can extrapolate from the extraordinary behaviors of subatomic particles, it stands to reason that parallel events and potentials are all are occurring simultaneously. Why don't we experience any of this? Our world is seemingly controlled by Newtonian mechanics. There aren't dead/alive cats. There are singular events. Why don't we experience quantum reality?

Today, a theory that makes the rounds among quantum physicists that when something gets bigger and bigger—remember these experiments are done on subatomic particles, the smallest isolated fragments of matter—when we pull back from a microscopic view of things, we experience what is known as "information leakage." The world gets less and less clear as it gets bigger; as we exit the subatomic level and enter the mechanical level that is familiar, we lose information about what's really going on.

American philosopher William James made the same observation in 1902. James said that when you view an object under a microscope, you're getting so much information; but more and more of that information is lost as you pan back. This is true of all human experience. A cohort of quantum physicists today says the same thing: that the actions of the particle lab are occurring around us always, but we don't know it because we lose information in this coarse physical world that we live in.

Neville said something similar. He said that you radiate the world around you by the persuasiveness of your imagination and feelings. A quantum physicist might call this observation. But in our three-dimensional world, Neville said, time beats so slowly that we do not always observe the relationship between the visible world and our inner nature. You and I can contemplate a desire and become it, but because of the slowness of time, it is easy to forget what we formerly set out to worship or destroy. Quantum physicists speak of "information leakage;" Neville basically spoke of "time leakage." Time moves so slowly for us that we lose the sense of cause and effect.

"Scientists will one day explain why there is a serial universe," Neville said in 1948, "but in practice, how you use the serial universe to change the future is more important."

# TRY

I want to leave you with a slogan of an American occultist P.B. Randolph who lived in New York City. He was a man of African-American descent and a tremendously original thinker and mystical experimenter. He died at the young age of 49 in 1875. This was his personal slogan: *TRY*. That's all. *TRY*. This slogan later appeared in letters signed by the spiritual masters Koot Hoomi and Morya, which started reaching Colonel Henry Steel Olcott in 1870s. The first appeared about two months before Randolph's death. The letters used the same slogan: *TRY*.

What you're hearing now is something to try. Neville's challenge was as ultimate as it was simple: "Put my ideas to the test." Prove them to yourself or dismiss them, but what a tragedy would be not to try. It's all so simple.

I want to conclude with words from William Blake, who was one of Neville's key inspirations later in life. Blake described the coarsened world of the senses that we live in. He described such things sometimes in matters of geography. When he would say England, he didn't mean England the nation exactly. He meant the coarse world in which men and women find themselves, the world in which we see so little, and the parameters close in so tightly that we don't know what's really going on. Then the poet would talk about Jerusalem, which he saw as a greater world, as a reality, created through the divine imagination, which runs through all men and women.

I want to close with William Blake's ode "Jerusalem" from 1810. I hope you'll try to hear these words as Neville himself heard them.

> And did those feet in ancient time
> Walk upon Englands mountains green:

*And was the holy Lamb of God,*
*On Englands pleasant pastures seen!*

*And did the Countenance Divine,*
*Shine forth upon our clouded hills?*
*And was Jerusalem builded here,*
*Among these dark Satanic Mills?*

*Bring me my Bow of burning gold:*
*Bring me my arrows of desire:*
*Bring me my Spear: O clouds unfold!*
*Bring me my Chariot of fire!*

*I will not cease from Mental Fight,*
*Nor shall my sword sleep in my hand:*
*Till we have built Jerusalem,*
*In Englands green & pleasant Land.*

# Questions and Answers

If there are a few questions, I'd be happy to take them.

**Speaker:** Can you do multiple wishes, say if there are three that you wish?

**Mitch:** Neville's own students in his lifetime asked him that very thing, and I'm in the same place myself because it's hard sometimes to limit one's wishes to one thing. Neville felt it was more effective if you limit it to one thing at a time; but he said that this was by no means a limit, you didn't have to limit yourself. The key thing is to feel the desire intensely and to hold your mental emotive picture with clarity and simplicity, and to stick with it. He did say he felt that at the time interval would be lessened if you limit yourself to one thing at a time. That was his practice, but he did not call it a must.

**Speaker:** I wanted something that didn't last, so to try to achieve that, do I meditate on it? How do I get result?

**Mitch:** Neville's idea was to enact a scene that would naturally transpire when the desired thing comes to pass. There may be many events that would transpire if that thing came to pass, but he said to select just one that has a particular emotional resonance, and then see yourself doing it over and over. Something as simple as a handshake or climbing a ladder. Just take one that has act emotional gravity and be persistent.

**Speaker:** Do you think that given his predilection for inner vision that there's any evidence suggest that Abdullah may have been a channel? Abdullah may have been a channel or a channel within Neville?

**Mitch:** Oh, that's an interesting question. He always referred to Abdullah as a flesh-and-blood figure, and he said Abdullah lived in an apartment on West 72nd Street, which I've visited, and he would talk about Abdullah in very physical, vivid terms, so he certainly described him as a flesh-and-blood being.

**Speaker:** You described many of the techniques, including the technique of walking in a cold winter day to get the feeling of being in another place. This is just other technique for the astral body. Basically, what he's describing is the emotional astral body being developed, of which one expression would be manifesting that state here, but it sounds like he could easily develop another technique because this sounds very limited.

**Mitch:** He does represent techniques such as walking and imagining himself in the palm tree-lined lanes in Barbados; but he most often came back to this idea of physical immobility and the uses of a hypnagogic state, that drowsy state. He again and again said that others can experiment, and should experiment, but that he personally found that to be the simplest and the most effective method. He would say sometimes he would enter the hypnagogic state and just feel thankful or try to seize upon one expression like *it is wonderful*. He might do that if he didn't have a specific thing that he was longing for at that moment. So he did experiment with some other techniques and points of view. He did said one lecture, "You praise others and you will shine," because it was very important to try to use these techniques to the benefit of another person. For example, if you have a friend who's looking for a job, you might form the mental picture of congratulating him or her on finding the perfect job because Neville believed in the oneness of humanity in the absolute most literal sense. There was no sentimentality about it. He felt that every individual was God.

**Speaker:** Did he say that he believed that the universe is holographic?

**Mitch:** He would say, and again, he sometimes made statements more in passing than full on, but he would say explicitly that we live in a universe of infinite possibilities, and everything that you desire, by the very fact of desiring it, because your imagination is a creative agent, already exists. It is a question of just claiming it, which is why it's so important to think from the desire fulfilled. It doesn't matter if you open your eyes or your checkbook or anything else and, of course, reality as we presently know it comes rushing back in. You must continue to think from the wish fulfilled, which he said was tantamount to selecting a reality that already existed. Schrodinger said there's a dead/alive cat. Neville would have said there are infinite outcomes and they all exist.

**Speaker:** Regarding the slowness of time, I'm curious what his thoughts were as far as the timetables for his technique.

**Mitch:** He said that we experience definite time intervals and that a time interval is part of the nature of our existence. I may want a new house and I may want that house right now, and I may think from the end of having that house, but he said, in effect, "The fact of the world that we experience here and now is that the trees have to grow to produce wood. The wood has to be harvested and the carpenter has to cut it. There will be time intervals." And he would say, "Your time interval could be an hour, it could be a month, it could be weeks, it could be years." There is a time interval. You nonetheless must stick to the ideal and try to make it just exquisitely effortless. He didn't endorse using the will. This isn't about saying, "I'm going to think this way." It is going into this meditative or drowsy or hypnagogic state, picturing something that confirms the realization of your desire, and feeling it emotionally; he said that when the method fails maybe it's because you're trying too hard. Neville wanted people to understand that there is an exquisite ease that one should feel with exercises.

**Speaker:** It sounds like he's saying that an emphasis on pure will would upset that balance.

**Mitch:** Yes. He used the word receptivity and he used the term time interval.

**Speaker:** Did Neville ever include other ideas outside of his system?

**Mitch:** He made very few references to other thought systems. He would frequently quote Scripture, mostly the New Testament. He felt the New Testament was a great blueprint and metaphor for human development in the figure of Christ. He felt that the Old Testament was suggestive of the promise and the New Testament was fulfilling of the promise, and beyond that he made little reference to other thought systems. He was chiefly interested in Scripture. He would talk about numbers; he loved symbolism. In his book *Your Faith Is Your Fortune* he talked about certain aspects of the zodiac, astrology, and number symbolism; but as time passed, he made fewer references to other systems. Every now and again he'd use a piece of language where I'll detect Emile Coué echoed; but so much of what we talked about really came from his own description of the world through his own experience. He made little reference to other systems.

**Speaker:** I started reading your book *Occult America* and there was a question in my mind—you write that a lot of positive thinkers and people in New Age in American history have, on the one hand, kind of advocated basic techniques and methods for selfish success and money, and, on the other hand, a lot of the better writers in New Age and New Thought were passionately involved with and concerned about social movements. Where did Neville fall in that dichotomy?

**Mitch:** That's a wonderful question and that was an aspect for me that made it difficult to first enter Neville's work, because he had no social concerns in the conventional sense, and if people raised social concerns, he would push them aside and would insist that the world you see, whether it is of beauty or violence, is self-created. Prove the theory to yourself and then use the theory as you wish. You want to eliminate suffering? Eliminate suffering. But he ardently rejected fealty to any kind of social movement or ideal. He believed that coming into one's awareness of the godlike nature of imagination, of the literal God presence of the imagination, of having the experience of being reborn through one's skull, was the essential human task.

**Speaker:** As you said in your own book, a lot the 19th century Spiritualists were involved in movements like suffragism and abolitionism.

**Mitch:** Yes. Well, you know, these radical movements, radical political movements and radical spiritual movements, avant-garde politics, avant-garde spirituality, they all intersect. We often fail to understand how a figure like Marcus Garvey, for example, was involved with mental metaphysics; but as you get closer to the real lives of these people, the connection becomes more natural because they craved a new social order both spiritually and socially.

# A Neville Goddard Timeline

**1905**: Neville Lancelot Goddard is born on February 19 to a British family in St. Michael, Barbados, the fourth child in a family of nine boys and one girl.

**1922**: At age seventeen Neville relocates to New York City to study theater. He makes a career as an actor and dancer on stage and silent screen, landing roles on Broadway, silent film, and touring Europe as part of a dance troupe.

**1923**: Neville briefly marries Mildred Mary Hughes, with whom he has a son, Joseph Goddard, born the following year.

**1929**: Neville marked this as the year that begin his mystical journey: "Early in the morning, maybe about three-thirty or four o'clock, I was taken in spirit into the Divine Council where the gods hold converse." (lecture from *Immortal Man*, 1977)

**1931**: After several years of occult study, Neville meets his teacher Abdullah, a turbaned black man of Jewish descent. The pair work together for five years in New York City.

**1938**: Neville begins his own teaching and speaking.

**1939**: Neville's first book, *At Your Command*, is published.

**1940–1941**: Neville meets Catherine Willa Van Schumus, who is to become his second wife.

**1941**: Neville publishes his longer and more ambitious book, *Your Faith Is Your Fortune*.

**1942**: Neville marries Catherine, who later that year gives birth to their daughter Victoria. Also that year, Neville publishes *Freedom for All: A Practical Application of the Bible*.

**1942–1943**: From November to March, Neville serves in the military before returning home to Greenwich Village in New York City. In 1943, Neville is profiled in *The New Yorker*.

**1944**: Neville publishes *Feeling Is the Secret*.

**1945**: Neville publishes *Prayer: The Art of Believing*.

**1946**: Neville meets mystical philosopher Israel Regardie in New York, who profiles him in his book *The Romance of Metaphysics*. Neville also publishes his pamphlet *The Search*.

**1948**: Neville delivers his classic "Five Lessons" lectures in Los Angeles, which many students find the clearest and most compelling summation of his methodology. It appears posthumously as a book.

**1949**: Neville publishes *Out of This World: Thinking Fourth Dimensionally.*

**1952**: Neville publishes *The Power of Awareness.*

**1954**: Neville publishes *Awakened Imagination.*

**1955**: Neville hosts radio and television shows in Los Angeles.

**1956**: Neville publishes *Seedtime and Harvest: A Mystical View of the Scriptures.*

**1959**: Neville undergoes the mystical experience of being reborn from his own skull. Other mystical experiences follow into the following year.

**1960**: Neville releases a spoken-word album.

**1961**: Neville publishes *The Law and Promise*; the final chapter, "The Promise," details the mystical experience he underwent in 1959, and others that followed.

**1964**: Neville publishes the pamphlet *He Breaks the Shell: A Lesson in Scripture.*

**1966**: Neville publishes his last full-length book, *Resurrection*, composed of four works from the 1940s and the contemporaneous closing title essay, which outlines the fullness of his mystical vision and of humanity's realization of its deific nature.

**1972**: Neville dies in West Hollywood at age 67 on October 1, 1972 from an "apparent heart attack" reports the *Los Angeles Times*. He is buried at the family plot in St. Michael, Barbados.

# About the Authors

**NEVILLE GODDARD** was one of the most remarkable mystical thinkers of the past century. In more than ten books and thousands of lectures, Neville, under his solitary first name, expanded on one core principle: *the human imagination is God.* As such, he taught, everything that you experience results from your thoughts and feeling states. Born to an Anglican family in Barbados in 1905, Neville travelled to New York City at age seventeen in 1922 to study theater. Although he won roles on Broadway, in silent films, and toured internationally with a dance troupe, Neville abandoned acting in the early 1930s to dedicate himself to metaphysical studies and embark a new career as a writer and lecturer. He was a compelling presence at metaphysical churches, spiritual centers, and auditoriums until his death in West Hollywood, California, in 1972. Neville was not widely known during his lifetime, but today his books and lectures have attained new popularity. Neville's principles about the creative properties of the mind prefigured some of today's most radical quantum theorizing, and have influenced several major spiritual writers, including Carlos Castaneda and Joseph Murphy.

**MITCH HOROWITZ** is a PEN Award-winning historian whose books include *Occult America, One Simple Idea, The Miracle Club,* and *The Miracle Habits*. His book *Awakened Mind* is one of the first works of New Thought translated and published in Arabic. The Chinese government has censored his work.

Twitter: @MitchHorowitz

Instagram: @MitchHorowitz23

CPSIA information can be obtained
at www.ICGtesting.com
Printed in the USA
JSHW052232161121
20522JS00005B/32